GERONIMO

Recent Titles in
Greenwood Biographies

GERONIMO

A Biography

Mary A. Stout

GREENWOOD BIOGRAPHIES

GREENWOOD PRESS
An Imprint of ABC-CLIO, LLC

A B C ⬤ C L I O

Santa Barbara, California • Denver, Colorado • Oxford, England

Library of Congress Cataloging-in-Publication Data
Stout, Mary, 1954–
  Geronimo : a biography / Mary A. Stout.
    p. cm. — (Greenwood biographies)
  Includes bibliographical references and index.
  ISBN 978-0-313-34454-1 (alk. paper) — ISBN 978-0-313-34455-8 (ebook)
1. Geronimo, 1829–1909. 2. Apache Indians—Kings and rulers—Biography.
3. Apache Indians—Wars, 1883–1886. I. Title.
  E99.A6G32744 2009
  970.004'97—dc22 2009031623

13 12 11 10 09   1 2 3 4 5

This book is also available on the World Wide Web as an eBook.
Visit www.abc-clio.com for details.

ABC-CLIO, LLC
130 Cremona Drive, P.O. Box 1911
Santa Barbara, California 93116–1911

This book is printed on acid-free paper ∞
Manufactured in the United States of America

This book is dedicated to the people who were here first.
May your stories continue to be told.
I also wish to thank my guys, Tom and Andy, for walking with
me as I retraced Geronimo's steps throughout southern Arizona.

There is properly no history; only biography.

—*Ralph Waldo Emerson*

CONTENTS

Photo essay follows page 60

SERIES FOREWORD

In response to high school and public library needs, Greenwood developed this distinguished series of full-length biographies specifically for student use. Prepared by field experts and professionals, these engaging biographies are tailored for high school students who need challenging yet accessible biographies. Ideal for secondary school assignments, the length, format and subject areas are designed to meet educators' requirements and students' interests.

Greenwood offers an extensive selection of biographies spanning all curriculum related subject areas including social studies, the sciences, literature and the arts, history and politics, as well as popular culture, covering public figures and famous personalities from all time periods and backgrounds, both historic and contemporary, who have made an impact on American and/or world culture. Greenwood biographies were chosen based on comprehensive feedback from librarians and educators. Consideration was given to both curriculum relevance and inherent interest. The result is an intriguing mix of the well known and the unexpected, the saints and sinners from long-ago history and contemporary pop culture. Readers will find a wide array of subject choices from fascinating crime figures like Al Capone to inspiring pioneers like Margaret Mead, from the greatest minds of our time like Stephen Hawking to the most amazing success stories of our day like J. K. Rowling.

While the emphasis is on fact, not glorification, the books are meant to be fun to read. Each volume provides in-depth information about the subject's life from birth through childhood, the teen years, and adult-hood. A thorough account relates family background and education, traces personal and professional influences, and explores struggles, accomplishments, and contributions. A timeline highlights the most significant life events against a historical perspective. Bibliographies supplement the reference value of each volume.

ACKNOWLEDGMENTS

I wish to thank Angie Debo, whose thorough and enlightened scholarship produced the definitive biography of Geronimo, which shines even more brightly thirty years after its initial publication. Her work remains unmatched and has served as the ultimate authority for this book. I wish our paths had crossed.

PREFACE

Geronimo is a name familiar to many, but few actually know much about his life and times. At the end of the 19th century, articles about his whereabouts and his exploits filled American newspapers, and settlers in the southwestern United States lived in terror of his name. One of the last remaining bands to be confined to a reservation, Geronimo's Apache people ranged freely throughout the southwestern United States and northern Mexico, raiding as they went. Eventually, the United States had to call on the full force of their military in order to capture Geronimo's tiny band, and even then, they could not accomplish the task without Apache scouts to assist them. Geronimo's ability to outwit the U.S. military for years, and his eventual capture and imprisonment, were the subjects of many newspaper and magazine articles and military memoirs of that era.

There is a large written record about Geronimo penned by his enemies, but even more interestingly, Geronimo lived long enough to have his autobiography published early in the 20th century. Such an account, of course, is central to any biography about the man. I have read and re-read his autobiography and pondered the difficulties involved in writing such an account through an interpreter, recorded by the hand of a stranger who was of the conquering culture, and published only with the permission of the U.S. military, while being held as a prisoner of war. Surely these conditions would have an effect on the words written and the truths revealed, but what kind of effect? Can we believe Geronimo's autobiography or not?

Fortunately, there are other corroborating accounts given by Apaches who were alive at the time, as well as the incomparable scholarship of Angie Debo, who published her definitive biography of Geronimo in 1976. These all tend to confirm the basic truth of Geronimo's autobiography, albeit a truth based on his own understanding of events and that differed from other people's truths. Factual errors were minimal, and questions arise more about that which was omitted from Geronimo's account, rather than that which it contains.

Geronimo remains as much a mystery now as when this journey began, although there is little doubt that such an intelligent, charismatic, and complex leader would have made a mark in the historical record during any time in which he lived.

TIMELINE: EVENTS IN
THE LIFE OF GERONIMO

ca. 1823   Geronimo born in No-doyoh Canyon near Clifton, Arizona.

ca. 1830   Geronimo probably begins his training as a warrior.

1830   Indian Removal Act passes Congress—the eastern tribes' land is taken in exchange for lands in Oklahoma, and the tribes are forced to move there.

Pre-emption Act passes Congress—settlers purchase "public lands" (including Indian territory) for $1.25 per acre, spurring westward migration.

1840   Geronimo is accepted as a full-fledged warrior and marries Alope, his first wife.

1846–1848   The U.S.-Mexican War is fought, resulting in a gain of more than 500,000 square miles of American territory from Texas to California. The *Apacheria* now belongs to the Americans, although the Apaches don't know this.

1851   Geronimo's mother, wife (Alope), and three children are killed by Mexican soldiers at Janos.

1852   Geronimo successfully leads a revenge battle against the Mexican army; he meets Americans for the first time. Geronimo marries his second wife, Chee-hash-kish, and soon after, his third wife, Nana-tha-thtith.

1883 Geronimo surrenders to General Crook at Cañon de los Embudos and returns to the San Carlos reservation.

1885 Geronimo flees the San Carlos Reservation into Mexico; his three wives, She-gha, Shtsha-she, and Zi-yeh are captured and returned to Arizona. Shtsha-she and one son, "Little Robe," die. Geronimo needs a wife, and marries Ih-tedda.

1886 Geronimo surrenders to General Nelson Miles at Skeleton Canyon; all the Chiricahua Apache prisoners of war are shipped to Florida. Daughter Lenna is born to Ih-tedda; She-gha's daughter dies.

1887 Geronimo's renegades are reunited with their families; all Apache prisoners are transferred to Mount Vernon, Alabama.

1889 Geronimo's last child, Eva, is born to Zi-yeh, his seventh wife.

1894 The Apache prisoners of war are transferred to Fort Sill, Oklahoma; Geronimo's son Chappo dies.

1897 Elbridge Burbank arrives to paint Geronimo's portrait, beginning a long association with the old man.

1898 Geronimo and others appear at the Trans-Mississippi and International Exposition in Omaha, Nebraska.

1901 Geronimo appears at the Pan-American Exposition in Buffalo, New York.

1904 Geronimo appears at the Louisiana Purchase Exposition in St. Louis, Missouri; his seventh wife Zi-yeh dies.

1905 Geronimo rides in Theodore Roosevelt's inaugural parade; he marries his eighth wife, Mary Loto.

1906 Geronimo's autobiography is published, and remains in print to this day.

1907 Geronimo marries his ninth wife, Azul.

1908 Geronimo's grandson Thomas (daughter Dohn-say's son) dies of tuberculosis.

1909 Geronimo dies of pneumonia at Fort Sill, Oklahoma.

Chapter 1

A CHILD NAMED GOYAHKLA

BIRTH OF GERONIMO

Though we will probably never know the precise date or place, sometime in the early 1820s, a boy child was born to Taklishim, son of the chief of the Bedonkohe band of Chiricahua Apaches, and Juana, an Apache of whom little is known other than her Spanish name, in a canyon near the headlands of the Gila River. A modern scholar has placed Geronimo's birth place near the present day town of Clifton, Arizona.[1] Geronimo's birth date, often given as 1829, has been proven incorrect by scholars (it was earlier in the 1820s), and his birth place, which he referred to as "No-doyohn Canyon," in Arizona, has never been located, although Geronimo most certainly knew where it was. Traditionally, Apache children were told where they were born and knew their birthplace despite the nomadic lifestyle of the band. Whenever the band's travels brought them back to the birthplace of a child, the child rolled on the ground toward each of the four directions. This traditional practice continued throughout the child's life and sometimes into adulthood.[2] The boy child born to Taklishim and Juana was named Goyahkla, the accepted translation being "He Who Yawns." It was an incongruous name for such an energetic man, who loomed larger than life and was probably at one time the most feared and best known American Indian in the southwestern United States.

Born into a close-knit Apache band consisting primarily of extended family members, Geronimo was probably attended by a midwife and female relatives at his birth. According to traditional custom, there would have been a cradle ceremony when he was about four days old, where a cradleboard, or *tsosch*, was carefully created just for him out of oak branches and sotol stalks by a shaman. Cradleboards usually had a canopy to protect the baby's face from the sun, and special items, such as a bag of pollen or a piece of turquoise, were hung from the canopy to protect the child. The baby did not actually use the *tsosch* for several months, until its neck was strong enough for the child to hold up his head. But the ritual placement of the new child into his cradle and the surrounding social ceremony welcomed a new child and expressed the tribe's hope that the child would live to occupy the cradle a few months hence.[3]

Although he didn't discuss it in his autobiography, it is likely that Geronimo also had a "First Moccasins" ceremony, given when a child began to walk. This event was marked with a feast of fruit and meat, and was overseen by a shaman who put pollen on the tiny ceremonial moccasins. These were placed on the child, who was usually between seven months and two years old, and with the assistance of a shaman, the young child was encouraged to walk a few steps into each of the four directions.[4]

Geronimo's father, Taklishim, was the son of Mahko, a chief of some repute in the Bedonkohe Apache tribe. Geronimo probably grew up hearing stories about the great chief Mahko from his father, admiring stories of battles, of prisoners and horses taken. The stories would probably have spoken of the vast lands that Mahko and his people ranged on horseback. These stories would have been repeated to the young Geronimo, who listened to them well, but little realized that his world would become an entirely different world—one that the great Mahko would never have recognized.

GERONIMO'S WORLD

Mahko was a great chief of the Bedonkohe band of the Chiricahua Apaches during a time when band members had never seen Europeans. There were great raids and battles, but these were against other bands of indigenous tribes, who were evenly matched with weaponry and technology. The *Apacheria*, the large area that was home to the Apaches, today encompasses the southwestern United States and northern Mexico. Originally, it was unsettled except for the Apaches, who lived a traditional lifestyle that involved spending summers in the mountains cultivating patches of squashes and melons among the forests and streams, and retreating to the desert valleys in the winter.

In 1830, the year that Geronimo probably began his training as a warrior, the Indian Removal Act was passed by the U.S. Congress, and authorized the U.S. government to negotiate treaties with the eastern tribes in order to take their land in exchange for lands in the West. This legislation resulted in the mass forced removal of American Indian tribes from the east coast of the United States to the west, disrupting traditional territorial boundaries, though the Apaches never faced too much indigenous competition for their remote part of the country, which consisted of stark high deserts dotted with "sky islands," or lush mountain biomes. During the same year, Congress also passed the Preemption Act, which allowed settlers to purchase for $1.25 an acre the public lands that they lived on and cultivated, spurring the westward migration of European settlers. That same year, Mexico restricted U.S. immigration into its northeastern province, which today is Texas, since the number of U.S. immigrants threatened to overwhelm the Mexican inhabitants. Clearly, the westward movement of the European Americans was reaching Arizona by the 1830s.

In 1852, when Geronimo fought against the Mexicans, they had already been defeated by the Americans in the battle for Texas, the Gold Rush had occurred, and the states of Texas and California had already joined the United States. It's no surprise that Geronimo met Americans for the first time that year. In all probability, the first Americans he met were government surveyors who were working on establishing the new border between the United States and Mexico in the aftermath of the war. Geronimo was inclined to like the Americans, as the Mexicans were his bitter enemies, but this feeling would soon change.

By the time the U.S. government began forcing the Apaches onto reservations in 1870, Arizona was a state, the Homestead Act was paying settlers to go west, the first transcontinental railroad had been built, the first national telegraph communications system had been built, and the

U.S. Army, having just finished fighting in the Civil War, was sent westward to fight the Lakota (Sioux), the Apaches, and any other American Indian tribe who wasn't peacefully settled on a reservation. Geronimo was middle-aged, and had more than 30 years of his life left to live.

During his last 30 years, Geronimo was captured once, surrendered several times, escaped many times, and finally lived out his life as a U.S. prisoner of war in Florida, Alabama, and Oklahoma, once there was nowhere left to run. He also rode in President Theodore Roosevelt's inaugural parade, appeared at the St. Louis World's Fair in 1904 as a major attraction, and published his autobiography. He never learned to speak English, but he dictated his memoirs through an interpreter, so that posterity had a record of his point of view. But he was never able to return to the homelands that he loved, the one thing he wished most for in his life.

GERONIMO'S TRIBE

Geronimo was born into the Bedonkohe band of the Chiricahua Apaches. The Chiricahua Apaches were nomadic and ranged in southeastern Arizona, southwestern New Mexico, and the northern states of Sonora and Chihuahua in Mexico. Their territory was south of the headwaters of the Gila River. East of the Bedonkohe were the Warm Springs (Ojo Caliente) Apaches, Victorio's band, who were friends with the Bedonkohes. Somewhat east, but closer, were the Mimbrenos led by Mangas Coloradas, whom the Bedonkohes regarded as chief while still retaining their own distinct identity. North of Geronimo's band lived the White Mountain Apaches. Geronimo mentioned that their bands didn't intermingle much and weren't friendly, but they weren't outright enemies. To the west, Geronimo named the Chihenne band, and to the south, the Chokonens, also referred to as the Chiricahua Apaches, Cochise's band, to whom Geronimo's band also looked for leadership during his lifetime. Southwest, in Mexico, resided the Nednai band that was most friendly with Geronimo's band due to family ties.

The Bedonkohes were familiar with their neighbors, and visited and traded with them. In many cases, the men and women of the bands intermarried, and the bands became close. Later during the Apache Wars, these bands often came to each other's aid, and ultimately were mixed together during capture and relocation. Geronimo became close friends with Juh, the leader of the Nednais, and regarded him as a brother.

APACHE WORLD VIEW

The Apaches believed in a life-giving deity called *Usen*, and Geronimo often referred to *Usen* when he explained his world view. Geronimo began his own autobiography with the creation story of the Apaches. In the beginning, as the story goes, the world was dark, and was ruled by the birds and the beasts. They fought, because the birds wanted to let in the light, and the beasts wanted the world to remain dark. The birds, whose chief was the eagle, won the war, which is why the eagle feather was a symbol of honor and courage for the Apaches. However, all human children were destroyed by evil beasts, the most fearsome being the dragon, until White-Painted Woman hid away one son, Child of the Water, in a deep cave. When the child came of age and wished to go hunting, he confronted the dragon who sought to destroy him. The dragon shot four arrows at Child of the Water, but was not able to hit him. Then the boy shot four arrows at the dragon, pierced his scaly hide, and killed him.

> This boy's name was Apache. *Usen* taught him how to prepare herbs for medicine, how to hunt, and how to fight. He was the first chief of the Indians and wore the eagle's feathers as the sign of justice, wisdom, and power. To him, and to his people, as they were created, *Usen* gave homes in the land of the West.[5]

The Apaches, similar to other tribal groups, believed in supernatural powers and shamans, tribal members who connected with the supernatural and created ceremonies for purposes of healing, confusing the enemy, improving hunting luck, and so on. The one large tribal ceremony for which the Apaches are best known is the girls' womanhood ceremony. This elaborate celebration of womanhood is still widely practiced among the Apaches today and involves days of instruction for the young woman, as well as gift-giving, feasting, and dancing in the evenings. Most tribal ceremonies happened on an as-needed basis, and often involved smoking, singing, special plants, foods, and use of colored paints. Ceremonies often made use of the number four: singing a song four times, smoking in the four directions, taking four bites of a special food. Geronimo himself was *not* a chief, as many believed. But he was a shaman with supernatural power that was recognized as being very strong, as well as a skilled warrior.

Geronimo believed that *Usen* gave homes to the people he created, and that the homes contained all the people needed to survive. The plants, animals, and birds they needed were there, and the people were to stay on the land made for them in order to survive.[6] This belief permeated the Apaches' world view; wrongdoers were not imprisoned as a punishment. The Apache society considered banishment from the band and its lands to be the strongest punishment. Ironically, Geronimo himself was forced to live away from his beloved homeland during his last years as a military prisoner of war, suffering the worst condition that his society recognized.

GERONIMO'S FAMILY

Geronimo was descended from the chief of the band, his grandfather Mahko. Apache leadership was not hereditary, but was based on ability. After Mahko's death, it is uncertain whether there was a successor. One Geronimo scholar says that Mahko was not replaced as chief of the Bedonkohe.[7] Geronimo's cousin, Jason Betzinez, says that Geronimo's father, Taklishim, succeeded his father as the band's leader.

Taklishim means "The Gray One" in Apache and Geronimo's mother was called Juana. This is a Spanish name, which could have indicated that she was from one of the southern Chiricahua Apache or Nednai bands, or may have been captured by the Mexicans sometime in her life.[8] Geronimo spoke Spanish later in life; whether he learned it from his mother or during his stays in Mexico is unknown.

Although Geronimo described his immediate family as consisting of three brothers and four sisters,[9] scholars note that the Apaches have only one word that means sibling or cousin, and don't distinguish between them. One scholar believes that Geronimo had only one sibling, a sister named Nahdoste, and that the rest of the "brothers and sisters" were actually cousins, all eight of them the grandchildren of Mahko by his two wives.[10]

APACHE CHILDHOOD

Geronimo's childhood was a typical Apache childhood. Once he grew enough to leave his *tsoch*, he probably played around the dwelling with his brothers and sisters, in the care of his mother or another female relative. He recalled playing hide-and-seek and mimicking the warriors by sneaking up on pretend enemies. At about age five, the children began helping the adults in the fields, about two acres cultivated and planted with corn, beans, and pumpkins, and also helped the women gather berries, tobacco, and other plants used by the people.[11] Girls also fashioned dolls to play with, and made miniature encampments. In adulthood, the girls would be responsible for making and breaking camp for the nomadic band, as well as cooking meals and caring for children. The boys created noisemakers, such as bull-roarers, and practiced hunting by flicking bits of mud from the ends of twigs at nearby songbirds. The children also began helping their parents with other daily tasks, which were differentiated by gender.

The young girls helped the women fetch water, harvest plants and foods, prepare meals, and create clothing. They also learned various twining and braiding techniques that could be used to make baskets.

The men were primarily hunters and raiders. Both hunting and raiding were acceptable activities for men. When they lived in their mountain camps, the men hunted animals. If their camp was located near a settlement, the Apaches were likely to raid it for food, horses, and women and children captives. Boys learned at a young age how to craft and shoot with bows and arrows, and all of the lore that goes with the hunt. They were trained to be tough and tireless runners. Older boys had to rise before dawn and run for miles holding a mouthful of water without swallowing it, or leap into icy streams. They participated in supervised wrestling matches and slingshot battles. They also learned to care for the band's horses. By the time they were 8 to 10 years of age, the boys began to actively participate during hunts. Geronimo enjoyed hunting, and thought that the most difficult animal to hunt was the deer, the primary game animal for the Apaches, although he also spoke of hunting antelope, elk, and, on occasion, buffalo. Even in his youth buffalo were difficult to find, and hunters had to travel long distances to find them on the southwestern plains. Turkeys and rabbits were also hunted regularly, but didn't require the discipline that deer required. Deer could only be approached downwind, related Geronimo, and often the hunters would take hours crawling on the ground, holding a bush in front of them to disguise their approach, before they were able to shoot a grazing deer.[12] They used the meat for food, and the tanned hides were used for teepees, moccasins, and other household items. According to Apache custom, there were taboo animals that were not hunted for food: bears, snakes, fish, and frogs.[13]

Tribal life was not all work. Various times and life events called for feasts, which Geronimo enjoyed, and he fondly recalled the feasts of his youth:

> To celebrate each noted event a feast and dance would be given. Perhaps only our own people, perhaps neighboring tribes would be invited. These festivities usually lasted for about four days. By day we feasted, by night under the direction of some chief, we danced. The music for our dance was singing led by warriors, and accompanied by beating the *esadadedne* (buckskin-on-a-hoop). No words were sung—only the tones. When the feasting and dancing were over, we would have horse races, foot races, wrestling, jumping, and all sorts of games (gambling).[14]

APACHE DWELLINGS AND FOOD

Apaches lived in wikiups, which suited their nomadic lifestyle well. They carried no lodge poles, but used the sticks, saplings, and brush on hand to construct the framework for low, rounded, igloo-shaped dwellings. The framework for a wikiup was covered with animal hides in the earlier days; later it was covered with cloth, or if the Apaches were on the run without many possessions on hand, with more brush or grasses. A hole was left in the center, and the fire in the dwelling was built in the dirt beneath the hole in the top. There was always one low entrance facing east, and sometimes a brush pile was placed in front of it to act as a windbreak and ensure privacy.[15]

In addition to the wild game that the men hunted, and which Geronimo spoke about, the Apaches also ate plant foods gathered and processed by the women of the tribe. Sunflower and other weed seeds, wild grasses, wild onions, mesquite beans, and cactus fruits were all part of the Apache diet. When the band was in the mountains, they gathered acorns and pinon nuts and ground them up along with hackberry seeds to make a paste that was cooked into a nutritious pancake. They also gathered wild berries and nuts, including wild walnuts. But the most important plant food for the Apaches was mescal, or agave. This was eaten much the way we eat an artichoke; the stalk was cut off and sometimes cooked, but the most desirable part was the heart of the agave plant. These hearts were gathered and roasted in a pit of heated stones, covered with grass, often for two to three days. Mescal, the cooked heart of the agave plant, was described as sweet and nutritious. It was either eaten immediately, or sliced and dried for later use.[16]

APACHE BELIEF SYSTEM

The Apaches believed in the life-giver *Usen*, who could be described as a god, but they had no form of organized religion. Their relationship with *Usen* was expressed through both personal and group prayer. Prayer was not used on formal occasions only, but permeated the daily walk of life. The Apaches used prayer in mundane daily events such as when they processed herbs into medicines; they also prayed before great undertakings such as raids, war parties, and hunts. Geronimo described the religious side of Apache life:

> We had no churches, no religious organizations, no sabbath day, no holidays, and yet we worshiped. Sometimes the whole tribe would assemble to sing and pray; sometimes a smaller number, perhaps only two or three. The songs had a few words, but were not formal. . . . Sometimes we prayed in silence; sometimes each one prayed aloud; sometimes an aged person prayed for all of us. . . . Our services were short.[17]

Supernatural power was recognized as a part of Apache life. Any Apache could receive supernatural powers at any time, although those who had recognized powers usually came into their powers after puberty. The power approached an individual through a word, sign, or animal form and asked if he or she wished to receive the power. If the person chose to accept the power, usually another experience occurred in a place that was special or sacred, which the anthropologist Morris Opler referred to as the "holy home." Here the ceremonies, words, and gestures that should be used were revealed to the person. The supernatural power was understood to be a power for good; its purpose was to heal, warn, and/or guard mankind. Therefore, the shamans who had a connection with a supernatural power were respected and called upon as needed in traditional Apache life.[18]

Geronimo came into his supernatural power as a young man. His power was recognized and documented in interviews with other Apaches who witnessed its use during his lifetime.

BECOMING A MAN

When Geronimo was a teenager, a group of Nednai Apaches who had Bedonkohe relatives came to visit. Among the rowdy young men was Juh, son of the chief and a known bully. He and his friends waylaid some Apache girls gathering acorns and teased them by snatching their full baskets of acorns. Geronimo's favorite cousin, Ishton, was one of the victims, and their grandmother instructed Geronimo to give Juh a good whipping. Although we don't know what happened between Geronimo and Juh at that point, we do know that Juh later became a Nednai war leader and returned to marry Ishton, Geronimo's favorite "sister" (cousin). He became part of the family, according to Apache custom, and Geronimo and Juh were close friends and comrades after that. Geronimo characterized Juh as a brother. Ishton and Juh went to live among the Nednais upon their marriage, as was customary.[19]

Sometime after Geronimo began hunting with the adults, his father died. His sister, Nahdoste, married Nana, a great chief of the Warm Springs Apaches, and his mother decided not to remarry, so young Geronimo undertook her support. Geronimo and Juana decided to visit Juh and Ishton down in Mexico, and left on a long and difficult journey together to a place they had never before visited. They had difficulties finding Juh's band, as they were so well-hidden. Geronimo was used to the peaceful *rancheria* life of his youth, which consisted primarily of hunting and farming. The Nednais, recognized as the wildest band of Chiricahua Apaches, lived an uncertain existence grappling with the encroaching Mexicans. After being driven from their native lands to the mountain strongholds, they began to rely more upon raiding as an economic necessity.

It was likely that, during his stay with the Nednais, Geronimo learned the fine art of raiding and had the opportunity to learn how to live secretly in the mountains: no visible teepees, running children, snorting horses, barking dogs, or smoking campfires gave away the location of the mountain Nednai camp. Geronimo would put these lessons to good use in later years.

Geronimo recalled that he was admitted to the Council of Warriors at the age of 17. Since his birth date is uncertain, this is a guess on his part, but is probably fairly accurate. He was a skilled, intelligent hunter who had the responsibility for caring for a parent at an early age. He very likely had experience raiding the Mexicans with the Nednai band during his visit there. He was probably ready for this step into adulthood. "When opportunity offered, after this, I could go on the warpath with my tribe. This would be glorious. I hoped soon to serve my people in battle. I had long desired to fight with our warriors," was his response to this event.[20] He remembered Chief Mahko's tales of the warpath, and saw himself following in his grandfather's footsteps. Geronimo had other motives as well. During his visit to the Nednais, he had fallen in love. Until he became a warrior, he could not take a wife.

NOTES

1. Angie Debo, *Geronimo: The Man, His Time, His Place* (Norman: University of Oklahoma Press, 1976), pp. 7–8. Although other historians speculate that he was born in New Mexico based on accounts from other Apaches, Debo believed Geronimo was quite aware of American political borders, and Geronimo said he was born in Arizona.

2. Morris Edward Opler, *An Apache Life-Way: The Economic, Social, and Religious Institutions of the Chiricahua Indians* (Lincoln: University of Nebraska Press, 1941), p. 10.

3. Opler, *An Apache Life-Way*, pp. 10–12.

4. Opler, *An Apache Life-Way*, p. 15.

5. Geronimo, *Geronimo's Story of His Life*, transcribed and edited by S. M. Barrett (New York: Duffield & Co., 1915), http://books.google.com/books?id=AvYaAAAAYAAJ, pp. 10–11.

6. Geronimo, *Geronimo: His Own Story*, as told to S. M. Barrett, newly revised and edited, with an introduction and notes by Frederick Turner (New York: Meridian, 1996), p. 57

7. Debo, *Geronimo*, p. 12.

8. Debo, *Geronimo*, p. 8.

9. Geronimo, *Geronimo: His Own Story*, p. 58.

10. Debo, *Geronimo*, p. 17.

11. Geronimo, *Geronimo: His Own Story*, p. 60.

12. Geronimo, *Geronimo: His Own Story*, p. 67.

13. Opler, *An Apache Life-Way*, pp. 326–332.

14. Geronimo, *Geronimo's Story of His Life*, p. 26.

15. Jason Betzinez, *I Fought with Geronimo* with Wilbur Sturtevant Nye (Lincoln: University of Nebraska Press, 1959), p. 29.

16. Betzinez, *I Fought with Geronimo*, p. 35.

17. Geronimo, *Geronimo's Story of His Life*, pp. 28–29.

18. Opler, *An Apache Life-Way*, pp. 200–216.

19. Betzinez, *I Fought With Geronimo*, p. 15.

20. Geronimo, *Geronimo's Story of His Life*, pp. 37–38.

Chapter 2

BECOMING GERONIMO

BECOMING A WARRIOR

According to Apache tradition, Geronimo had to assist on at least four raid or war expeditions before being accepted as a full-fledged warrior by the band's council. During these expeditions, young initiates didn't fight, but prepared camp, gathered wood and water, cared for the horses, and stood on guard duty at night. This customary apprenticeship prepared young men for the risks and rewards of the warrior's life without full participation.

A young man became a novice or initiate by volunteering to accompany a raid or war party. He was instructed before he left by his father, male relative, or a war shaman, for four days. Similar to the young women who underwent the womanhood ceremony, the novice was associated with the supernatural during the time he accompanied a raiding or war party, as befitted a manhood initiation for the young Apache males. As a novice, a young man was referred to as "Child of the Water," and was required to observe behavioral and food restrictions. He ate cold food, was forbidden to eat intestines, drank through a tube made from a plant stalk, carried a scratcher, and used ceremonial words while on the raid or war expedition. The novice led the expedition until the band arrived at the location where they would carry out a raid or an attack. The cap worn by the novice was different from the warrior's, which contained eagle feathers. The novice's cap contained eagle down, oriole down, quail feathers, and hummingbird feathers to ensure his swiftness.

During the most dangerous expedition activities, the novices were protected and required to stay far away from the action and watch the actual battle or raid. However, they did participate in the hardships of the expedition itself and fulfilled their role within the expedition. After completing his fourth trip as an apprentice, a young man was able to join a raid or war party as a full-fledged adult the fifth time. If a young man's behavior or demeanor was found lacking as a novice, he was simply not invited to participate in any additional trips.[1]

MARRIAGE AND MASSACRE

Geronimo didn't mention his training in his autobiography, only the joy of achieving warrior status at the early age of 17. Right after Geronimo became a warrior, he returned to the Nednais to arrange his marriage to a young woman, Alope. Alope's father, Noposo, requested quite a large number of horses, which caused Geronimo to speculate that either he wanted to keep his daughter, or he didn't care about their love. Perhaps he wasn't fond of the brash young warrior, who flouted tradition by arranging his own marriage instead of leaving such arrangements to relatives, as was customary. Whatever the reason, Geronimo left the Nednai camp after meeting with Noposo, only to return in a few days with the herd of horses named as the bride price. Alope packed her belongings and followed her new husband to his camp, where Geronimo had set up a new teepee next to his mother's, and they were officially married. Geronimo wrote that they lived a happy, traditional life and were raising three children as Geronimo had been raised, with love and patience.[2]

In 1850, the state of Chihuahua, Mexico issued an invitation to the Apaches to come in peace to trade. The Bedonkohes, now under the leadership of Mangas Coloradas, chief of the Mimbreno Apaches, decided to travel south to take advantage of the trading. They received cloth, knives, and beads in trade for the cattle, horses, and mules they had acquired on raids, probably against the Mexicans in neighboring Sonora, who were considered to be the enemies of the Nednais, just as the Chihuahuans were friendly. The Bedonkohes were camped outside a settlement in Mexico that Geronimo referred to as Kaskiyeh, but was probably Janos, not far from Casas Grandes in Chihuahua. Since this was a peaceful trading expedition, the open camp contained the women and children who accompanied the party, while the men traveled daily into town to drink and trade. On March 5, 1851, while the men were in town, a contingent of 400 soldiers from Sonora, led by Colonel Jose Maria Carrasco, crossed the boundary into Chihuahua and surprised the camp, killed the few remaining guards, and took horses, supplies, and Apache prisoners.[3] During the raid by the Mexican soldiers, those not captured or able to escape were killed by the soldiers. Carrasco's army invaded two camps that day, killing 21 Apaches and capturing 62. Some of the fleeing women and children met the warriors returning from town to tell them the horrific tale of the unexpected attack and slaughter of the band by Mexican soldiers. According to Apache war strategy, all survivors scattered and hid, then returned silently to a predetermined location at nightfall to gather and discuss their next steps. Geronimo waited silently, hoping against hope as the remaining Bedonkohes arrived one by one at the rendezvous. As the evening wore on, the horrible truth became clear—he had lost his mother, wife Alope, and all three children in the raid. Hatred burned in his soul. This massacre of his loved ones became the defining moment in Geronimo's life; it set him on his life's path. He swore vengeance on the Mexicans, and from that day forward his life was governed by his unceasing hatred of the Mexicans and his thirst for revenge. It's possible that the Mexicans offered the treaty and peaceful trading opportunity as a trick, to lull the Apaches into thinking there was no danger and to set them up for the horrendous massacre. According to one account, the trading included free mescal (an alcoholic drink) supplied by the Mexicans.[4]

A DIFFERENT POINT OF VIEW

There is another scholarly account of this raid that has been pieced together from the Mexican newspapers of the time, and from Carrasco's memoirs. It represents a different point of view—that of the Mexican soldiers. In the years preceding the event, the Apaches' raids in northern Sonora and Chihuahua had become so fierce that the regions became depopulated. Mines, haciendas, and ranches were abandoned after Apaches raided, taking livestock, supplies, and sometimes prisoners for ransom. The dangers of living in northern Mexico, coupled with the lure of the California gold fields, encouraged the Mexican settlers to give up and move away. As they did, the Apaches ventured further inland to raid, as this had become a subsistence activity for them. Raiding was simply an economic necessity because there was no better way to survive.

The two northern Mexican states dealt with the problem in different ways. Chihuahua sought to sign peace treaties with the Apaches in order to curb their depredations. The Apaches were willing to sign the peace treaties as long as they included rations. Once signed, they honored the treaties, counting the Chihuahuan Mexicans as friends, and the Sonoran Mexicans as enemies. They cleverly confined their raids to Sonora, and sold the livestock and goods obtained by the raids to the Mexicans in Chihuahua.

However, the Sonoran government, equally as desperate as Chihuahua to stop the Apache raids, selected a different solution. They contacted the national government and requested soldiers to protect them from the Apaches. The Mexican army soldiers, who served the whole country, felt they were not bound by the borders of the individual states, and crossed into Chihuahua to punish the Apaches who had signed the peace treaty and were openly living near Janos. This massacre of the friendly Apaches by the army was protested by the governor of Chihuahua, as it violated his treaty and he feared reprisals, but to no avail.[5] This tangle of Mexican politics and the differences in the lifestyles and cultures of the Mexicans and the Apaches presented unsolvable problems for everyone. The Mexicans were settling on lands the Apaches used to call their own. As Apache hunting and farming lands became more restricted, the Apaches adapted to the new situation by raiding the newcomers to make up for the lost hunting and farming. In the beginning, raiding might also have resulted in more food for less effort than it took to bring down a deer or patiently tend a patch of melons. It was a situation bound to lead to conflict, and it did. The Apaches, who experienced years of conflict with the Mexicans, retreated to their mountain strongholds and to their more wide open northern territories. However, history soon repeated itself as the Americans began their westward movement, presenting exactly the same issues that the Apaches experienced with the Mexicans. But by the time the Americans arrived, the Apaches knew better how to resist the newcomers, having learned from the Mexicans.

APACHES AND DEATH

There is another mystery about the Janos massacre. Regardless of which side's version is accurate, Geronimo lost his family that day, and it changed him forever. However, there is no indication that the band members that met at the rendezvous returned to the camp site to positively identify the bodies of the dead. There were captives taken and sold as slaves to the interior of Mexico according to Carrasco, so how did Geronimo know that his family was among the dead and not enslaved? Geronimo said nothing of this in his own account of the massacre. As an old man, Geronimo was painted by artist Elbridge Burbank, who recounted that Geronimo said he had seen his family all dead, lying bloodied on the ground after he returned from town.[6] One reason the warriors probably didn't return to the camp site to mourn and bury the slain had to do with the Apaches' traditions surrounding death and the dead. If Geronimo returned to verify that the bodies of his family were in the camp, it was in violation of a taboo, so it's not surprising he never mentioned it. According to the anthropologist Morris Opler, the Apaches feared death. Dead people were buried quickly in unmarked graves, which were never revisited, lest the dead person's ghost be present. Apache ghosts had an alarming tendency to linger in the area where they died, or where they were buried, which explains the cultural traditions around death. Bodies of the dead were buried as quickly as possible facing the sunset (west). Their clothing and possessions were either buried with them or burned, so as to free them for use by the deceased in the underworld and to discourage ghosts from returning to their material possessions. Survivors even avoided saying the names of the dead aloud, or grieving too much, lest they inadvertently draw the ghosts to themselves. It was believed that proximity to a ghost would cause ghost sickness, and that malicious ghosts might also appear as owls in order to exert evil influence. The symptoms of ghost sickness included loss of consciousness, extreme weakness, fear and terror, and vomiting. It was necessary to have a shaman complete an appropriate ceremony to rid a person of ghost sickness.

Geronimo related that upon returning home, he burned his mother's teepee and all of her possessions in accordance with tradition. He also burned his wife's and children's' possessions, including their toys, and he even went so far as to burn his own teepee that he had shared with his family.

Another reason the Apaches simply left after the massacre was that they understood that it had been an act of war, and they were deep in the enemy's territory unprepared for battle. They had no weapons or supplies, and they were surrounded by the Mexicans. Later on the day of the massacre, the Bedonkohe warriors gathered for a council, and Geronimo took his place, but did not speak or vote. The council decided to return home immediately, and Mangas Coloradas, the great Apache chief, ordered the band to begin the trip. Geronimo stood as his band began the trip home, not knowing what to do. He finally followed them at a distance, not eating or speaking to anyone. His loss and his grief were so extreme, he was numb.

GERONIMO'S POWER

It was during this time of grief that Geronimo received his supernatural power. As he sat, alone and bereft, he heard a voice call his name four times. Then the voice told him, "No gun can ever kill you. I will take the bullets from the guns of the Mexicans, so they will have nothing but powder. And I will guide your arrows."[7] Indeed, Geronimo was shot and wounded many times in battle, but he was never killed. He always fought with confidence and ferocity, believing in the power that had been given to him and that stayed with him throughout his lifetime.

Geronimo was described as a medicine man, and there are numerous anecdotes about Geronimo being called upon to heal sickness throughout his life. When this sickness was caused by interaction with coyotes, wolves, or dogs, Geronimo's coyote power ceremony was performed to cure the sickness. One eyewitness account described such a ceremony. When Geronimo was an old man, a patient came to his home and lay in front of a roaring fire near an arbor at sundown. Geronimo sat facing east, with the patient in front of him, and held an old black basket filled with an abalone shell, an eagle feather, and a bag of pollen. He lit a cigarette and puffed smoke in each of the four directions. Then he rubbed pollen over the patient's body and prayed as he did so. Next, he sang songs, accompanying himself with a curved stick on a small drum. Many of the songs were about Coyote, and how he was a tricky fellow, hard to find and to see. Geronimo talked about how he also had been given these characteristics, and how the coyote power helped him heal people with the coyote sickness. He ended his songs with a coyote howl. This ceremony was repeated four nights in a row.[8] Geronimo presided over other ceremonies as a medicine man throughout his life. He was reputed to have cured ghost sickness, and also to have had a gun ceremony, where he shared his personal power. Those who underwent a gun ceremony could never be killed by a gun.

REVENGE

After the Bedonkohes returned home in the wake of the massacre at Janos, Mangas Coloradas held another council of the warriors, who wanted revenge on the Mexicans. After the Council agreed on a course of action, Geronimo's task was to visit the surrounding bands to see if their warriors would join the Bedonkohes on the warpath. He visited the Chokonen Apaches, headed by the great chief Cochise, who agreed to join the Bedonkohes against the Mexicans. Then Geronimo traveled south to visit the Nednais and Chief Juh, who also agreed to help.

Warriors were never forced to join a war expedition; participation was always voluntary, and each warrior decided for himself whether to participate in any given war expedition. However, the recruiting technique used by the Apaches for building their volunteer armies was the war dance, and it was very effective. The dance was organized by band leaders, including shamans, and served as a means of committing the warriors to the enterprise and supporting the warrior's expedition spiritually.

Betzinez, Geronimo's cousin, described a huge council called by Baishan, the principal chief of the Warm Springs Apaches, which included the chiefs of the surrounding bands. Once the plans for the expedition to Mexico were agreed upon, the chiefs jointly announced a great war dance, which made an impression on Geronimo's young relative. The purpose of the war dance, as he described it, was to ". . . recruit volunteers for the expedition and to stir up a fighting spirit."[9] First, an enormous bonfire was built, and singers chanted and drummed on one side. The dance began with four men dressed for war, who entered from the east and danced around the fire four times. Well-known warriors were called to pace around the bonfire as their bravery was praised and their exploits recounted. Warriors stepped from the crowd to join the war leader of their choice and danced, becoming a part of the expedition. Other men signaled their intention of joining the war party by pacing around the fire. As the dance went on, often a shaman would sing a song, naming a warrior and calling him to join. Few could refuse this personal appeal, and joined the dance around the fire.

Following the dancing, the warriors shot guns, bows, and arrows over the heads of the singers in a sham attack. This demonstrated how they would fight in the actual battle. Excitement and morale were high, and the warriors were jubilant as they celebrated. The war dance was more than a recruitment method and a morale booster. It was also a very religious experience, where men danced for power and prayed for safety. They smoked and blew smoke to the four directions, praying that they would kill an enemy.

After the completion of the four day celebration, the warriors prepared for the expedition. They made new spears, bows, and arrows, and the few Apaches who owned guns replenished their ammunition. Bows were usually made of mulberry wood and strung with twisted sinew. Arrows were made of plant stalks and fletched with turkey feathers. The preparations took awhile, and it was some time before the bands gathered on the border in full war gear. They removed their shirts and folded them under their belts, ready to fight in breechcloths and moccasins. As they set out to inflict revenge on the Mexican troops, the band of warriors was 175 strong.

The warriors dressed for battle were an imposing sight. There was no prescribed way to paint their faces for battle, but Geronimo was reported to have painted the faces of the warriors that fought with him with white paint, marking foreheads, cheeks, and noses. Whether shamans used war paint as directed by their power for spiritual purposes or to help prevent the warriors from shooting each other is a matter for speculation.[10] Perhaps both reasons were valid; friendly fire was as much a problem for the American Indians in battle as it continues to be in modern warfare. Each warrior traveled on foot, wearing only a breechcloth around his waist, moccasins, and a buckskin headband. He carried only enough food for three days, as well as his weaponry: bows, arrows, spears, and knives. Geronimo acted as guide as they traveled about 40 miles a day. They headed toward Arispe, where the Mexican troops were located. Their families were hidden in a mountain camp to await their return.

There was a small skirmish the day the Apaches arrived, but the following day, the entire Mexican force met the Apache warriors on the battlefield. As Geronimo described the conflict, he was allowed to direct the Apache forces since he had been the most deeply wronged. He positioned the various Apache warriors in a semicircle in the trees near the river so they could surround the approaching Mexican forces. Geronimo chose to lead them in a pitched battle against the two companies of Mexican cavalry and two infantry companies, rather than employ the usual guerilla tactic of an ambush from a hidden position. "I thought of my murdered mother, wife, and babies—of my . . . vow of vengeance, and I fought with fury," said Geronimo in his autobiography.[11] The Apache warriors won the day, fighting with bows and arrows and spears in close combat, against the Mexican army's rifles and cannons. A swift running Apache warrior armed with a spear could run up to a Mexican regular after he fired a shot from his rifle, and run him through before he could reload. The field was strewn with Mexican and Apache casualties, although the Mexicans suffered a total defeat in this battle.

THE MYTH BEGINS

Although none of the firsthand accounts of the battle mention it, tradition and folklore relate that during this battle, Goyahkla's name became Geronimo. No one really knows how Goyahkla received the name Geronimo, but the story is that he fought so fiercely against the Mexicans that some cried out for Saint Jerome repeatedly during the battle. The conclusion was that the repeated cries of Geronimo during the battle so aptly led by that furious warrior somehow became associated with him, and people began to refer to him as Geronimo, a practice he encouraged.

Geronimo's ferocity as a warrior, and his legendary status as a human tiger, began during this battle. The battle satisfied the band's need for revenge, and they traveled north to home. Geronimo, however, was not satisfied, and continued to seek revenge upon the Mexicans.

NOTES

1. Morris Edward Opler, *An Apache Life-Way: The Economic, Social, and Religious Institutions of the Chiricahua Indians* (Lincoln: University of Nebraska Press, 1941), pp. 134–139; Grenville Goodwin, *Western Apache Raiding and Warfare,* edited by Keith Basso, (Tucson: University of Arizona Press, 1971), pp. 288–298.

2. Geronimo, *Geronimo: His Own Story,* as told to S. M. Barrett, newly revised and edited, with an introduction and notes by Frederick Turner (New York: Meridian, 1996), p. 71.

3. While the date of the massacre of Geronimo's family is most often given as 1850, Sweeney's article using Mexican sources dates the massacre to 1851.

4. Jason Betzinez, *I Fought With Geronimo* with Wilbur Sturtevant Nye (Lincoln: University of Nebraska Press, 1959), p. 3.

5. Edwin Sweeney, "'I Had Lost All': Geronimo and the Carrasco Massacre of 1851," *Journal of Arizona History* 27, no. 1 (Spring 1986), pp. 35–52.

6. Elbridge Ayer Burbank, *Burbank Among the Indians* as told to Ernest Royce. (Caxton Press, 1972), http://www.harvard-diggins.org/Burbank/Burbank_Among_The_Indians/Burbank_Among_The_Indians.htm, p. 17.

7. Angie Debo, *Geronimo: The Man, His Time, His Place* (Norman: University of Oklahoma Press, 1976), p. 38.

8. Opler, *An Apache Life-Way,* p. 40.

9. Betzinez, *I Fought With Geronimo,* p. 4.

10. Opler, *An Apache Life-Way,* p. 344.

11. Geronimo, *Geronimo's Story of His Life,* transcribed and edited by S. M. Barrett (New York: Duffield & Co., 1915), http://books.google.com/books?id=AvYaAAAAYAAJ, p. 52.

Chapter 3

FIGHTING THE MEXICANS

THE RAIDING LIFESTYLE

Although Geronimo settled back into his life after the battle against
the Mexicans that gave him his name, he was restless to return to Mexico and fight again. By then he had married again: his second wife,
Chee-hash-kish, was a member of his own Bedonkohe band, and was
described as "handsome." Geronimo married her soon after Alope's
death, and she remained married to him for 30 years until her capture by Mexicans in 1882. Geronimo's son, Chappo, was born to her
in 1867, and his daughter Dohn-say (also called Tozey or Lulu), was
born in 1871. He also married a third wife, Nana-tha-thtith, during
this time, as was customary for a good provider and successful raider.
Apache men were allowed to marry as many women as they could support, and through the years Geronimo added and discarded wives as
circumstances dictated, leaving historians with an incomplete record
of his domestic life.

There is no doubt that his previous battle at Arispe was primarily
for revenge against the Mexican soldiers for the massacre of his family and friends, but like any Apache on the warpath, Geronimo never
returned home without booty—stolen horses, weapons, clothing, and
other goods. The spoils were expected after any raid or attack, and
sustained his growing family. He soon convinced two other warriors,
Ah-koch-ne and Ko-deh-ne, to travel into Mexico and attack a village

there and steal some horses. As they closed in on the horses, the Mexicans opened fire from inside the surrounding houses, and Geronimo's two companions were cut down. Geronimo managed to escape, and headed back to Arizona with the Mexicans in pursuit on horseback. He retreated home, running and hiding, never stopping for food or rest, and arrived home alone and without booty. He had failed.[1]

"But my feelings toward the Mexicans did not change—I still hated them and longed for revenge. I never ceased to plan for their punishment, but it was hard to get the other warriors to listen to my proposed raids."[2] During the 1850s, Geronimo continued to lead raids into Mexico, sometimes with as few as two other warriors. Some raids were successful, others were not. He attacked mule trains loaded with provisions, as well as a company of Mexican cavalry. Many times he returned to Arizona wounded, once smashed in the head by a rifle butt, another time shot in the side. There were times when he returned with nothing except losses, and the people blamed him, but he continued to raid in Mexico and gradually built a reputation as a cunning, ruthless fighter.

One time, while Geronimo stayed in camp nursing his wounds from a raid, most of the others went on a trip north to trade with the Navajos for blankets. As morning dawned, three companies of Mexican soldiers who had surrounded the camp during the night opened fire, and the remaining Apaches scattered for cover, running for their lives. Nana-tha-thtith, Geronimo's third wife, and their child were killed during the attack, and Geronimo managed only to let fly a single arrow, killing a Mexican officer, before he ran and hid. The Mexican soldiers took all the horses, weapons, blankets, and goods that they could carry and burned the teepees and everything else they contained. Winter was coming and the band was left unprepared. Four women captives were taken back to Mexico after the raid, including Geronimo's cousin and Jason Betzinez's mother, Na-thle-ta.

Her story is an amazing but typical Apache captive story. After being taken to Chihuahua to work for a family, Na-thle-ta was transported by wagon to Santa Fe after she was sold to a wealthy Mexican who lived there. She managed to escape, and walked more than 250 miles back to camp, existing on nuts, berries, seeds, and whatever else she could find as she traveled home.[3]

After that attack, Geronimo had more family deaths to avenge, and he returned to his raiding life in Mexico with redoubled effort. The following summer, Geronimo and eight other men successfully attacked and captured a pack train filled with supplies, including blankets, calico, saddles, tinware, and sugar. Upon their return through Tucson, Arizona, they came upon a mule train loaded with cheese, headed for California. They took this, too, when the lone American driver fled, and returned to camp, where the great chief Mangas Coloradas held a celebration to fete the successful warriors and divide the spoils among the tribe.

The Apache interactions with the Americans could be generally characterized as friendly and infrequent, and the Apaches approved of the war between the United States and Mexico. In 1848, the Treaty of Guadalupe Hidalgo ended the U.S.-Mexican War and transferred Mexican territory in the southwest, including California, to the United States. In 1854, the United States acquired much of present-day Arizona and New Mexico from Mexico through the Gadsden Purchase. Geronimo's first interaction with Americans may well have been with the men who surveyed and established the border with Mexico after the Gadsden Purchase, and some miners. Geronimo initially had a very positive impression of the Americans, and reserved his hatred for the Mexicans.

RAIDING HIGHLIGHTS AND LOWLIGHTS

Accounts of Geronimo's raids on Mexico during this time are numerous. On one raid, his party successfully stole a mule train filled with bottles of mescal (an alcoholic drink made from a type of agave plant). When the raiders stopped for the night, Geronimo became alarmed when he realized that every warrior was becoming drunk on the mescal, and that Mexican soldiers might be in pursuit. Worse, the warriors began arguing and fighting with one another. Somewhat inebriated himself, Geronimo poured out all of the remaining mescal, removed the mules to another location further away, doused the camp fires, and stopped the fighting. He tended to the wounded, cutting out one arrow head and one spear point from the most grievously wounded, then kept guard all night long. As the raiding party staggered wearily home the next day, they stumbled upon some cattle that had strayed from a herd, and somehow managed to drive them back home with them. An exhausted Geronimo had managed to create success from disaster, increasing his reputation as a wise leader and ruthless warrior. Geronimo reported that this was the first cattle the Apaches had ever tasted, and they determined to go and capture more. From this time forward, the focus of raids included cattle herds in addition to horses and mules.[4]

Not all of Geronimo's raids were successful; in fact, some were disastrous. One raid even had all of the markings of a comedy. One year, when they were not expected (the Apaches having not raided in Mexico for awhile), Mexican troops surprised Geronimo's camp by arriving in force, rounding up all the Apaches' horses and mules, and driving them south. Geronimo and 20 other warriors had to pursue on foot, since all their horses had been taken. After the warriors found the horses at a Sonoran cattle ranch, the men attacked and killed two Mexicans, and retrieved their livestock, which they began driving back to Arizona. They were trailed by nine cowboys from the ranch, who intended to take the horses back again. One night, Geronimo and his men waited until the Mexican cowboys slept, then cut loose the cowboys' horses, added them to their own herd, and continued their journey back to Arizona, leaving the cowboys asleep, unharmed, and without mounts. Geronimo said he didn't know what happened to the cowboys, but he considered it a "good trick" to get their horses and leave the men asleep in the mountains.[5]

When the raids were successful, the band ate well; when they were disastrous, the band went hungry. The raids brought not only food and horses to the Apaches, but also new goods and new technologies. A raided pack train might produce cloth, clothing, pots, pans, and other household goods, as well as mules to eat and horses to ride and trade. And while the Apaches commented critically that the whites had a lot more "stuff" in their homes and in their lives, they began to desire the additional goods as well. Even so, the relations between the Apaches and the Americans remained amicable, and there were frontier accounts of large herds of cattle being driven through Apache lands without being disturbed at all. Indeed, it was reported that the Apaches helped the American cowboys find water holes and other necessities on their journey and were satisfied with the payment of a couple of steers for their assistance. Thus far, the Apaches had preserved their good relations with the Americans by confining their raids to Mexico and their avowed enemies.

GERONIMO AND COCHISE

During this time, Geronimo married his fourth wife, She-gha, a relative of Cochise. He was now bound to Cochise by family ties, and supported him in his upcoming fight against the U.S. Army. She-gha's brother, Ya-nozha, became one of Geronimo's staunchest warriors. Somewhat later, Geronimo married his fifth wife, Shtsha-she, from his own Bedonkohe band. Little is known about Shtsha-she, even though she stayed with him through his capture and captivity.

In 1855, the U.S. government appointed Dr. Michael Steck as the Indian agent for the southwestern tribes, and he lost no time in approaching all the bands with treaties that included provisions for government control over their lands. Geronimo remembered making a pact of nonaggression with the American soldiers. He told of himself, Cochise, and Mangas Coloradas shaking hands and promising to be brothers to the American soldiers in his autobiography. But at that point in time, none of the Apache leaders realized the full implications of the treaties, specifically, the enormous land cessions. They remembered the promises to remain friends and allies, but were unaware of the fine print in the treaties, in which they relinquished rights to their own lands.

In 1856, the U.S. Army built its first fort in the *Apacheria*: Fort Buchanan, located near present-day Tubac, Arizona. The soldiers there were charged with keeping the peace with the Apaches in the new U.S. territories and keeping the travel routes open. There were plans afoot to establish a railroad route through the area, and miners were beginning to come into the new U.S. territory, drawn by discoveries of silver, gold, and copper in the Gadsden Purchase area.

In 1858, the Butterfield Overland Mail from St. Louis, Missouri to San Francisco, California ran twice weekly through Chiricahua Apache country at Apache Pass. The California Trail was becoming a major east-west overland route through the new American territory, and in order to ensure adequate water and supplies for travelers, ran through

the heart of the Apache territory. More and more Americans were beginning to come west, and they were coming through Apache country,
many of them headed to the gold fields in California. During the same
year, Steck met with the Chiricahuas, and though he acknowledged
that they had not broken a treaty with the Americans during the past
two years (they continued to raid only in Mexico), history tells us he
already planned to move them to the Gila River area along with the
Mimbreno, Mogollon, and Mescalero bands.[6]

Trouble began when the miners began moving in to Apache country
to open copper mines, and a gold strike created the mining town of
Pinos Altos, which sprang up practically overnight in the Gila Wilderness in 1859, deep within the territory of the Mimbrenos. The miners
were greedy, lawless, and wild, and encouraged the Mexicans to build
settlements around the mines to feed the miners and support their en-
deavors. In 1860, Fort McLane was established close to Pinos Altos
(located near modern-day Silver City, New Mexico) and Indian Agent
Michael Steck planned to establish a Mimbreno reservation away from
Pinos Altos. His report for that year indicated that the influx of Americans and Mexicans had drastically reduced the hunting available to
the Mimbrenos, and the introduction of alcohol was having a negative
effect on the band.

Mangas Coloradas, Mimbreno chief, and, at that time, the leader of
all of the Chiricahua Apaches, went alone on a friendly visit to Pinos
Altos against the wishes of Geronimo, Victorio, and Loco, the latter
two important leaders of the Warm Springs Apache bands. Mangas
Coloradas was notable for his size; he was described as over six feet tall
and a clever and astute statesman. He quickly expanded his leadership role beyond the Mimbreno, or Copper Mine band, by marrying
his daughters to leaders of neighboring bands, thus creating a strong
alliance that the Apaches had not previously experienced.

Mangas Coloradas listened as the other leaders begged him not to
trust the miners, but he visited anyway, only to be tied to a tree and
whipped with bullwhips by the miners. Although he escaped with his
life, the miners ultimately did not. Mangas Coloradas ended his peace
with the White Eyes, as the Americans were called by the Apaches,
as a result of the careless and cruel bullying he suffered at the hands
of the miners. The first ally he called upon to join him was his son-

in-law, Cochise, who up to that point had been instrumental in keeping the Butterfield stage route open and safe through Apache Pass, his Chokonen band providing firewood for the stage company. And since Geronimo was, through his fourth wife, kin to Cochise, he soon became involved as well.

The Apaches raided Pinos Altos, taking all the crops and livestock and killing anyone they could find. When the mining settlement was demolished, they began attacking and raiding the wagon trains on the California Trail and defending against the retaliatory raids by the miners on the Apache *rancherias*. The miners turned the tide of the Apaches' good will toward the Americans, causing Mangas Coloradas to call on all his relatives and allies to go to war with the White Eyes. Although Geronimo may have participated in this fighting, it didn't take place near the Bedonkohe *rancheria*. It took Lt. George Bascom to bring the fight closer to home, and to ignite the all-out war between the Apaches and the Americans that didn't end until Geronimo's final surrender.[7]

THE "CUT THROUGH THE TENT" AFFAIR

In 1861, an unknown Apache band raided a small run-down ranch near the Chiricahua Mountains in Arizona, taking the livestock and a young boy who was herding the animals. This raid was erroneously attributed to Cochise, who was summoned by Lt. Bascom to his tent in Siphon Canyon, near the Apache Pass station. Lieutenant George Bascom was sent from Fort Buchanan to Apache Pass with 54 men to find and recover the child. Bascom invited Cochise and his family into his tent, where he accused Cochise of kidnapping the child, and ordered the child returned. Lt. Bascom said he would keep Cochise's family as hostages until Cochise returned the boy. Cochise replied that he didn't have the child, but would try to find him. Later it was discovered that the raiding band had given him to a White Mountain Apache band, where he was raised until he later joined the U.S. Army as an Apache translator and tracker under the name of Mickey Free.

When Bascom attempted to take Cochise into custody, he whirled, sliced open Bascom's tent with his knife, and made good his escape. He instantly raided first the Butterfield station, then one of the stagecoaches at Apache Pass, and took his own hostages, immediately offering to trade his hostages for Bascom's. What actually happened, and when, is a mystery that historians are still figuring out.

A later (1872) newspaper interview of Cochise by Arizona's Governor Safford purports to give Cochise's account of the incident, but contains inaccuracies. In the article, Governor Safford described Cochise as about six feet tall, with long black hair mixed with gray, and about 60 years of age, his face smooth and sad. Safford described Cochise's shirt, breechcloth, headband, and moccasins and told of how he and Cochise had gone to Cochise's camp, where one of Cochise's three wives prepared a supper of baked cakes, boiled beef, coffee, and sugar. After eating, according to Safford, Cochise described the incident from his point of view. He said that Lieutenant Bascom had invited him and his family into his tent to enjoy his hospitality, saying nothing was wrong and that his unit was just traveling through. Once inside the tent, Cochise noticed that it was suddenly surrounded by soldiers. Bascom told him that he and his relatives would be held as prisoners until they gave up the little boy. Cochise protested that he could not give up the boy as he did not have him, and, waiting for the opportunity, cut a hole in the tent and escaped. Gathering reinforcements, Cochise immediately returned to the Apache Pass station, where he took his own prisoners, including the hapless station master and some passengers on a passing coach. He returned to Bascom and offered to exchange prisoners, but Bascom refused unless the young boy was returned. After reaffirming that he didn't know the whereabouts of the boy, Cochise returned a final time with the station-keeper, a rope tied around his neck and looped around Cochise's saddle horn. The station-keeper begged Bascom to make the prisoner exchange, but Bascom was steadfast in his refusal. Cochise dramatically wheeled his horse around, and spurred him away from the camp at top speed, dragging the station-keeper by the neck.[8]

Although the stationmaster didn't survive as Cochise's hostage, he was not dragged to death as described in the dramatic, but wildly inaccurate newspaper article. Indeed, Cochise had every hope of saving his relatives by exchanging hostages. The stationmaster had been an acquaintance who voluntarily came to Cochise to try to resolve the problem, but had been kept as a hostage to be exchanged. A day later, Cochise held up a passing stage to increase his number of hostages to match those held by Bascom. He even had one of his American hostages write a note that said, "Treat my people well and I will do the same by yours, of whom I have four."[9] The note was placed on a bush on a hill near the soldiers' camp. Cochise continued to try to convince Bascom to trade hostages, but to no avail. Bascom stubbornly refused to trade his hostages for anyone other than the boy he had been sent to recover, to the despair of the local White Eyes and even some of his own troops. One soldier who questioned his decision was court-martialed.

Cochise was backed into a corner, and time was running out. Suspecting that probably more troop reinforcements were on the way, he gathered his allies and attempted to rescue his family by attacking the soldiers, but the soldiers were able to withstand the attack with some casualties on both sides, and Cochise failed to rescue his family. Although Cochise sent out runners to query other Apache bands, he never found the young boy; instead, the situation degenerated rapidly.

At that point, Cochise wasn't sure whether his relatives were still alive, and the families of the warriors who had died in the attack on the soldiers were allowed to have the four hostages to kill. Their bodies, riddled with lance wounds, were found by the soldiers, who then had to determine the fate of their own hostages. Bascom was reluctant to execute his hostages, but Lt. Moore, who had arrived with reinforcements and outranked him, insisted, and the Apaches were hanged from a tree near where the bodies of the tortured Americans had been found and buried. Those executed included Cochise's brother and nephew, who had just completed his warrior training. The Americans released Cochise's wife and child. That child was Naiche, who eventually became the chief of Geronimo's band. The incident, referred to as the "Cut through the Tent" affair or the "Bascom Affair," ignited the Apache Resistance, a period of war and bloodshed between the Apaches and Americans that lasted from 1861 until Geronimo's final surrender in 1886.[10]

Geronimo described this incident and the succeeding fallout laconically in his autobiography: "After this trouble, all of the Indians agreed not to be friendly with the white men any more. There was no general engagement, but a long struggle followed."[11]

THE CIVIL WAR

Geronimo and his Apache brothers soon became embroiled in the American Civil War, although they had barely begun to learn that the

Americans believed they owned the lands that the Apaches had lived on for untold generations. After the southern states seceded from the United States of America and declared themselves a separate entity, the Confederate States of America, the Confederate troops began to move throughout the South to consolidate their territory, and soon moved west. The Butterfield stagecoach route, much of it established in Confederate territory, was abandoned and moved to the Overland Trail route through Wyoming and Nebraska. Stations in New Mexico and Arizona were abandoned. Soon the U.S. government began closing the military posts and forts established in the southwest, and Indian agent Michael Steck left the area as well.

With the abandonment of the military posts and their protection from the Indians gone, the miners fled, and the settlers who supported the miners in nearby towns began to leave, too. Mangas Coloradas took this opportunity to attack the mining town of Pinos Altos and drive away the remaining miners and settlers. The Apaches celebrated, feeling that at last they had driven away the greedy whites who were encroaching on their territory. Little did they know that a Confederate colonel named John Robert Baylor was on his way, having named himself the military governor of their territory. In March of 1862, the Indian-hating Baylor issued orders to exterminate all hostile American Indians. The method he suggested was to lure them in to peace negotiations, and then kill the adults and sell the children to Mexicans. The Confederates, established in Tucson, Arizona eastward through El Paso, Texas, never got a chance to act on these treacherous orders, because Union soldiers from Colorado and California were coming to rout the Confederates.[12]

The Apaches continued to attack all white military outfits indiscriminately, and the next key battle took place at Apache Pass. In July 1862, General James Henry Carleton took his Union soldiers in the California Column through the pass on their way to New Mexico, where they ran out Baylor's Confederates. The troops had to go through Apache Pass to get water from the spring there, having marched 40 miles in the grueling heat from the San Pedro River with only their morning coffee to sustain them. They were not expecting to meet the Apaches as they approached the pass in a long, straggling line.

The Apaches, organized by Mangas Coloradas and Cochise, carefully planned their ambush, hiding above the abandoned Butterfield station.

From their hiding places, the Apaches carefully shot the Union troops as they came through the pass. They felt that with their superior numbers and position, they could surely win the battle. The thirsty troops, who had long since emptied their canteens, were desperate to reach the spring and replenish their water. Inspired by Sergeant Albert Fountain, his unit charged the high ground at Overlook Ridge, where Apaches rained down deadly gunfire. Using their mountain howitzers to shell the Apaches on Overlook Ridge, Fountain's unit was able to take the high ground, which turned the battle. The Union troops were able to rout the Apaches, who scattered to their mountain strongholds.[13]

This battle was significant because it was the first time the Apaches had been well-armed with rifles—rifles they had taken from defeated or killed American troops. This was an indication of a major shift in the two years since the Apaches had begun to fight the White Eyes, as they referred to the Americans, in earnest. The California Column achieved their objective, but in order to reach the spring had to bring out the big mountain howitzers and blast their way through the pass, pushing back the Apaches under fierce shelling that they had never before experienced. The California Column finished their march to the Rio Grande without further incident, although Carleton was horrified as the column marched on, passing burnt wagons, skeletons, and graves that testified to the efficiency of the Apaches' war on the White Eyes.

Carleton took military control of the Apaches' territory, and his policies regarding the American Indians proved to be as unrelenting as Baylor's. He immediately began the construction of Fort Bowie near Apache Pass, recognizing, as did the Apaches, the military value of this key pass. Whoever controlled the pass could control the flow of commerce and travel throughout the southwestern United States.

Carleton set about to control or exterminate all the American Indians in his area of command. He herded the various Indian tribes onto small, military-controlled reservations. After the Navajos and the Mescalero Apaches were moved to the tiny, barren Bosque Redondo reservation where they fought and starved, Brigadier General West was assigned to move the other Apache groups (whom he called Gilas) onto a reservation. Carleton issued orders to West to fight and kill the Indians as he found them. In particular, Mangas Coloradas's Apache band was selected to be the first order of business; Carleton directed

West to begin a campaign against Mangas. At that time, it was thought that Mangas Coloradas's band was active in harassing the miners at Pinos Altos, so General West sent an expedition into that area in January 1863.[14]

NOTES

1. Angie Debo, *Geronimo: The Man, His Time, His Place* (Norman: University of Oklahoma Press, 1976), pp. 48–49.

2. Geronimo, *Geronimo's Story of His Life*, transcribed and edited by S. M. Barrett (New York: Duffield & Co., 1915), http://books.google.com/books?id=AvYaAAAAYAAJ, p. 57.

3. Jason Betzinez, *I Fought With Geronimo* with Wilbur Sturtevant Nye (Lincoln: University of Nebraska Press, 1959), pp. 19–24.

4. Debo, *Geronimo*, p. 53.

5. Geronimo, *Geronimo: His Own Story*, as told to S. M. Barrett, newly revised and edited, with an introduction and notes by Frederick Turner (New York: Meridian, 1996), p. 101.

6. Debo, *Geronimo*, pp. 55–56.

7. Debo, *Geronimo*, p. 61.

8. A.P.K. Safford, "Cachise: Governor Safford's Account of His Interview with the Apache Chief—The Career of Cachise from the First Hostilities—His Present Desire is for Peace," *Chicago Daily Tribune*, December 24, 1872.

9. E. R. Sweeney, *Cochise: Chiricahua Apache Chief* (Norman: University of Oklahoma Press, 1991), p. 156.

10. Debo, *Geronimo*, pp. 62–63.

11. Geronimo, *Geronimo's Story of His Life*, p. 118.

12. Debo, *Geronimo*, p. 66.

13. E. R. Sweeney, *Mangas Coloradas: Chief of the Chiricahua Apaches* (Norman: University of Oklahoma Press, 1998), pp. 429–440.

14. Lee Myers, "The Enigma of Mangas Coloradas' Death," *New Mexico Historical Review* 41:4 (October 1966): p. 289.

Chapter 4

FIGHTING THE AMERICANS

THE MURDER OF MANGAS COLORADAS

The next major event in Apache history, which Geronimo called "perhaps the greatest wrong ever done to the Indians . . .," was the murder of Mangas Coloradas, which took place on January 19, 1863.[1] While not the initial trigger for the relentless war between the Apaches and the White Eyes, it was the event that signaled the point of no return for the Apaches. After the battle at Apache Pass, Mangas Coloradas, who was probably near 70 years old, desired peace with the Americans, and requested a treaty. Lulled by a promise of peace, Mangas Coloradas, after convening a great council of all the bands, including his Mimbrenos and the Bedonkohes, concluded that the bands should remove to Pinos Altos, called Apache Tejo by Geronimo, and live in peace, drawing rations from the U.S. government. This offer was made by the citizens and soldiers living there when Mangas Coloradas and three warriors went to speak with them. The citizens and soldiers invited the tribe to settle there, and said they would be issued blankets, provisions, beef, and supplies. At the council, it was decided that Mangas Coloradas and about half the people would go to New Mexico and settle near the White Eyes. Geronimo, ever mistrustful, stayed in Arizona with the rest of the people. At approximately the same time that Mangas Coloradas was in council with the Apaches, arguing for peace with the Americans, General Carleton issued his General Order Number

1, which, among other things, directed General West to embark on a mission to "chastise" Mangas Coloradas's band of Apaches.[2]

Though alert and well-armed, Mangas Coloradas was eager for peace in January 1863, and headed to the abandoned ruins of Fort McLane, where a group of American prospectors under Captain Joseph Reddeford Walker were camped with Jack Swilling, a former Arizona Guard officer. The Americans hatched a scheme to capture Mangas Coloradas and keep him as a hostage to ensure their safe passage through the *Apacheria*, when they were joined by General West's advance guard of 20 soldiers under Captain Shirland. The groups joined forces and flew a white flag to bring in Mangas Coloradas. They hid the soldiers. Jack Swilling went out to speak with Mangas Coloradas and urged him into camp, where he was surrounded by the soldiers. Mangas Coloradas dismissed his bodyguard, which consisted of Victorio and one of his sons. Swilling told Mangas Coloradas that he would be held hostage to see Swilling's party safely through the territory. Mangas Coloradas led the party to the abandoned Fort McLane, where they met General West and the main body of the troops.[3]

Once in the clutches of the California Volunteers, Mangas Coloradas was disarmed and kept under guard, told that only his compliance would ensure the safety of others in his camp. The venerable chief was described as having ". . . prominent, bloodshot eyes and . . . was a head and shoulders above any paleface present . . . He had a head of hair that reached his waist. His nose was aquiline and was his one delicate feature, both in size and form. His receding forehead was in keeping with his receding jaws and chin. His wide mouth resembled a slit cut in a melon, expressionless and cruel."[4] Military reports show that Mangas Coloradas was subsequently shot to death while attempting to escape. While four separate eyewitness accounts to this incident disagree as to the particulars, and as to whether he was tortured before his death, it seems likely that the California Volunteers were looking for an excuse to execute Mangas Coloradas. Although it cannot be proven, General West may have even ordered Mangas Coloradas's death that night. One believable account tells that one of the guards waited until Mangas Coloradas slept, then threw a large rock against the wall of his roofless adobe cell. Startled by the sound, Mangas leapt to his feet, only to be shot to death by his two guards, who subsequently reported his attempted escape.[5] Another account by Daniel Conner, a member of Walker's civilian group who claimed to be an eyewitness, says that the soldiers guarding Mangas Coloradas heated their bayonets in the campfire where Mangas lay wrapped in a blanket, and teased him by touching his naked legs and feet with the burning iron. Goaded, Mangas Coloradas told the soldiers in Spanish that he was no child to be toyed with, whereupon the sentinels shot him to death.[6] General West's official report of the incident is filled with lies. He claims that his troops captured Mangas Coloradas, that the Apache attempted to escape three times that night, and that the sentries shot him to death on this third escape attempt.[7]

Regardless of the exact circumstances of his death, there is some agreement about the shameful handling of Mangas Coloradas's dead body. It seems that he was decapitated by the army surgeon, his head boiled in a large cooking pot, and his skull sent back east to a phrenologist, who reported that it was larger than Daniel Webster's skull, and used it as a lecture exhibit.[8] Conner went on to say that one soldier came and scalped the dead body with a Bowie knife, and then the soldiers lifted his body on the blanket, dumped it in a ditch, and covered it with a foot and a half of dirt.[9] The Apaches were horrified by this treatment, since it meant that Mangas Coloradas would continue to be brainless and headless in the afterlife.

After his death, the soldiers quickly attacked the two camps of Apaches that had accompanied Mangas Coloradas. Geronimo, having heard nothing from the Mangas Coloradas group, assumed foul play and moved his camp farther away, but to no avail. They were attacked by the soldiers, scattered, and regrouped with Cochise and his Chiricahua Apaches. They were attacked again, and scattered again. Mangas Coloradas's decimated band joined with the Warm Springs Apaches, and Geronimo, now leading the Bedonkohes, joined forces with Cochise and the main Chiricahua Apache band.

In the meantime, Steck returned as Indian agent, with plans to relocate all of the Apaches onto reservations, to acculturate them, and to encourage them to farm and accumulate property. Simultaneously, General Carleton continued with his plans to mercilessly eliminate every Apache male and imprison all females and children. It was not at all unusual in the western United States for the federal Bureau of

Indian Affairs, administered by the Department of the Interior since its transfer from the War Department in 1849, and the military to be operating in the same territory with different, or even conflicting goals. While neither group had the best interest of the Apaches in mind, clearly wanting to move them out of the way of the onslaught of westward migration at any cost, it's easy to imagine how confusing it was for the Apaches, who heard a different story from every pair of lips. In addition, there existed the very real danger of mistranslation, since most communication took place in limited and broken Spanish unless an Apache translator was present. Although Apache translators became more common as the U.S. military began to hire Apache scouts, the personal motives of the scouts often colored the translations.

AFTER THE CIVIL WAR

During the post-Civil War period, miners and settlers continued to move west in increasing numbers. Pinos Altos was populated by miners again, and a silver strike established Silver City, New Mexico. Though there were intermittent efforts to establish treaties with the Apaches and/or to confine them on reservations, the bands, for the most part, raided and killed as need or opportunity struck. Frontier newspapers were filled with accounts of Apache raids, and the pressure on the government intensified along with the Apache depredations. For example, the February 12, 1870 issue of *The Weekly Arizona Miner*, in an article titled "Protection Badly Wanted for Arizona," described Arizona Governor Safford's journey to Washington DC to ask for additional military protection from the Apaches:

> Of all the American Indian tribes, the Apaches are indisputably the worst. They are monsters of revenge and cruelty, practicing refinements of torture upon captives compared with which the worst horrors of the Spanish inquisition were mild.... Within the last two years, their successes have emboldened them, and their raids upon small white settlements have been more daring and bloody than ever. According to a tabular statement, one-ninth of the able-bodied white population has been killed, wounded,

or missing in engagements with Apaches within the last eighteen months.[10]

In 1871, the fearful and enraged citizens of Tucson, Arizona took matters into their own hands. Frustrated with the inability of the military to protect the citizens from the Apaches, a group of vigilantes from that town banded together with the local Papago (Tohono O'odham) Indians and Mexicans, and attacked a group of peaceful Apaches settled at Camp Grant outside the city, resulting in a massacre of between 125 and 144 innocent Apaches while they slept. Since most of the men were away on a hunting trip, the vast majority of the dead were women and children; approximately 30 infants were taken and sold into slavery in Sonora. The shocked military set about burying the mutilated corpses of the Apaches, and President Grant threatened to place Arizona under martial law if the perpetrators were not brought to trial. More than 100 men were indicted and brought to trial in Tucson, where a jury subsequently found them all not guilty after deliberating for 19 minutes.[11]

THE PEACE MISSION

Largely as a result of the Camp Grant Massacre, the federal government instituted its new Peace Policy in Arizona, which called for settling all Apaches on reservations near military forts to protect them from the citizens and encouraging them to learn to make a living through agriculture and raising livestock. In 1871, the U.S. Congress established a fund for purchasing land and settling the Apaches on reservations. In the same year, the military assigned General George Crook, America's foremost Indian fighter, to round up the Apaches in the southwestern United States once and for all. True to form, the Interior Department assigned an Indian Agent, Vincent Colyer, to the southwest, where he proceeded to contact and establish peaceful relations with the Apache bands, one by one, before Crook could get to them. After contacting band leaders, Colyer set up reservations near military forts closest to the bands' home lands. General O. O. Howard, assigned to a peace mission with the Apaches by President Grant himself, went out to accompany the bands to the reservations, and he broadcasted his peaceful intentions widely. Much to Crook's disgust, General Howard contacted Cochise first and got his agreement to move to the Alamosa reservation, before Crook could engage him in combat. Crook had identified Cochise as the worst of the Apaches, and was determined to go after him first.

Cochise was able to work with Howard and to convince him to establish a reservation that encompassed the Chiricahua and Dragoon Mountains in far southeastern Arizona, and to name as the Indian agent Thomas Jeffords, a person familiar to and trusted by the Apaches. After 11 days of talks, the 1872 treaty established the Chiricahua reservation and allowed the Apaches living there to draw rations. Geronimo was pleased with these arrangements, although he remained wary about trusting the American general. When the negotiating party traveled to meet the soldiers, infantry and warrior alike were surprised that Geronimo chose to ride behind General Howard on the general's horse, Geronimo's arms around Howard's waist. Some Apaches may have interpreted such a gesture on his part as approval; others may have thought that Geronimo was clever to keep his enemy close— surely, if the situation deteriorated, no U.S. soldier would try to shoot him and thereby endanger his senior officer. Geronimo settled near the Fort Bowie agency near Apache Pass with Cochise, and they gave up their lives of raiding in the United States in order to draw supplies from the fort. Their raiding trips into Mexico also dwindled. Often their Warm Springs (Ojo Caliente) relatives came to stay with them. It was a relatively peaceful time in Geronimo's life. He and Cochise admired General Howard because he had lost an arm, and because he prayed for peace prior to meeting with them. The Apaches probably thought that Howard's survival from such a great wound showed his power, and they approved of the concept of praying before a large undertaking, something the Apaches did before each and every raid or battle.

AGENT CLUM

Fort Bowie during those times often saw Cochise and his two sons, Taza and Naiche, visiting and interacting with the soldiers. They kept their word; Cochise's people (including Geronimo and the Bedonkohes) never broke the peace or raided within the United States. However, Arizona's Governor Safford received complaints from Sonora, Mexico regarding Apache raids, and the American federal government struck a course with the Apaches that would soon undo the temporary peace.

The Tonto, the Yavapai, the White Mountain, and the Coyotero Apache bands were all confined to the barren San Carlos reservation, which was run by Agent Clum, who arrived in August of 1874. Referred to by the Apaches as Turkey Gobbler for his posturing and displays, Clum enjoyed his position and remained convinced that he could save the U.S. government money if he could confine all the Apache bands to a single reservation (the San Carlos, which was run by him, of course). Clum was quick to express this opinion to everyone, which created concern among the southern Apache groups that they might not be able to keep their beloved Chiricahua reservation, which suited them well.

Unfortunately, Cochise died in 1874, which was a devastating loss for the Apaches. He was a strong and respected leader, and had the power to speak for the bands, and the power to negotiate. He had trained his eldest son, Taza, to be a leader as well. Naiche, although well-liked, was fond of gambling and good at making friends, but had difficulty making decisions and being a leader. On his deathbed, Cochise instructed both sons to never break the peace with the Americans, and he appointed Taza his successor.

On October 30, 1876, just four years after the Chiricahua reservation was established, it was revoked by order of President Ulysses S. Grant, and the Apaches then living there were to be escorted to the San Carlos reservation. At the time, Taza's, Geronimo's, and Juh's bands were living on the Chiricahua reservation fairly peacefully, although they continued to raid and attack occasionally in Mexico.

THE FIRST ESCAPE

However, an incident that started the chain of events that led to the loss of the Chiricahua reservation began with Cochise's death. Skinya, one of Cochise's warriors, refused to accept Taza as the new band leader, and a splinter group of Cochise's band left the agency to live in the nearby Dragoon Mountains.[12] After they were sold liquor by a Califor-

nia Trail station keeper at Sulpher Springs, Skinya's warriors became
intoxicated and went on the warpath, killing the station keeper and
stealing horses and ammunition. The military chased them back into
the Dragoon Mountains, but were unable to find them. This led to
hysterical headlines in the Tucson newspaper, and Arizona's Governor
Safford wired Washington DC and requested the closing of the Chiricahua reservation. The irony that the cooperative Apaches were being
punished for the actions of a band of renegades not even located on
the reservation was lost on the government. The outcome of the Chiricahua reservation closure was probably the opposite of what the local
citizens would have wanted. Closing the reservation resulted in several
bands of the most dangerous Apaches being scattered throughout the
area with no oversight, where no one could find them, and in dire need
of food and supplies to sustain them.

Agent Clum, with military support, arrived on June 4, 1876 to remove the Apaches at the Chiricahua reservation to the San Carlos
reservation. He met with Taza, who agreed to bring his band to San
Carlos. Geronimo and Juh then asked to meet with Clum to make
arrangements for the Bedonkohes and the Nednais to be removed to
the San Carlos reservation. Geronimo spoke, and Clum assumed that
he was chief, not realizing that Geronimo often spoke for Juh, who
had a speech disability, but who was actually the chief. Geronimo told
Clum that he wanted his people to go to San Carlos, but that they were
camped about 20 miles away, and asked for permission to get them and
return to Clum. Permission was granted, and Geronimo, Juh, and another warrior, Nolgee, rode swiftly to camp. They shouted orders, and
the Apaches packed swiftly and killed their dogs so that barking would
not give them away, and Juh and Nolgee rode toward Mexico. By the
time Clum's men, who had followed them to camp, rode back to inform
the military, Juh and Nolgee's bands were in the Sierra Madre Mountains in Mexico, preparing to hide out in familiar territory. Geronimo
and about 40 of his band rode east and turned up at the Warm Springs
reservation to stay with relatives. This was the first of Geronimo's many
escapes from government capture.[13]

As the other Chiricahua bands prepared to make the trek to the
San Carlos reservation, counts taken at the beginning and end of
the trip indicated that many of the Apaches had slipped away during

the journey to San Carlos, probably to make their way south and join other Apache bands.

RESERVATION LIFE

When John Clum took over as the Indian Agent at the San Carlos reservation in August 1874, approximately 800 Indians resided there. Clum actively pursued a policy to consolidate the Apaches at San Carlos from the time of his arrival, and by August 1875, only one year later, there were 4200 Apaches living at San Carlos.[14] The crowded conditions and the fact that many of the different bands represented were enemies were not taken into account. The reservation itself was described as barely habitable, even by the soldiers stationed there. The various bands concentrated in the flats near the San Carlos River near what is today Globe, Arizona, were from different parts of the southwest. Many bands came from the mountains, and found the crowded, hot conditions in the steamy flatlands intolerable. The Apaches were not allowed to hunt or to make *tizwin*, their traditional alcoholic drink. The reservation was noted for its mosquitoes, and often diseases caught from the soldiers, such as smallpox, swept through the crowded camps and resulted in many deaths. The situation was further exacerbated by lazy, uncaring government agents, who either participated in or tolerated the enormous fraud practiced by the government contractors who supplied the rations to the reservation Indians. A grand jury investigation into one Indian agent detailed how government contractors were paid for supplies not delivered to the reservation, and how profits were divided by the government contractors and the Indian agent, while the Indians were poorly fed. The document went on to describe the incredible power the Indian agents had over the lives of the people on the reservations, and how they abused that power.[15]

John Clum probably didn't participate in the fraud so commonly practiced by the Indian agents and federal contractors. In fact, he established his own "personal body-guard and free-lance army," as he described it, by putting 54 Aravaipa and Coyotero Apache Indians on the government payroll as the reservation police. He was quite proud of his police force, and on the way to the Chiricahua reservation to bring in Cochise's people, he stopped off in Tucson and gave the citizens of that town quite a show. Clum said that the Tucsonans requested a performance, and he asked his police force to put on a genuine war dance. On the appointed evening, a large campfire was lit in the center of the Military Plaza, and Clum's police force appeared in traditional garb, armed with lances and shields, bows and arrows, or rifles loaded with blanks issued by Clum. Three thousand people arrived to watch them dance accompanied by singers and drummers. The performance became more frenzied, the war whoops louder and more shrill, and the Tucsonans more alarmed, veterans that they were of actual Apache attacks. At the culmination of the dance, the Apaches with rifles began firing blanks over the audience's heads, and the crowd scattered as they ran out of the plaza. Clum gleefully reported that ". . . the play was becoming a bit too realistic to suit the fancy of the average 'pale-face.'"[16]

Clum's enthusiasm led to some less-than-wise decisions, including one to take 22 Apaches back east in 1876, including young Chief Taza. Clum attempted to cover his travel expenses and enter show business by putting on a "Wild Indian Show" similar to the one he had treated the Tucsonans with. He debuted at the Olympic Theater in St. Louis, but his timing was bad. His show, coming mere weeks after Custer's slaughter by the Sioux in Montana, was a bust. The party continued on to the Philadelphia Exposition and Washington DC, where Taza got sick and died of pneumonia. After having him buried back east in an elaborate funeral ceremony, Clum obtained funds from the Commissioner of Indian Affairs to pay for return travel expenses, and accompanied the Apache group to Colorado, where he sent them on to Arizona on their own. He headed back to Ohio, where he married Mary Dennison Ware and brought her back to the San Carlos reservation, where she was the only white woman.[17]

Although ill-prepared, Naiche became Chief upon his brother's death when Clum and the other Apaches returned to San Carlos. Due to his basic honesty and competence, Clum was able to weather the whispers that he poisoned the former chief. Geronimo and his band were certainly aware of the conditions at San Carlos, and were not eager to be relocated to that reservation. So, with their assigned reservation gone, Geronimo simply decided to join the Warm Springs (Ojo Caliente) Apaches on their reservation, which was more appealing to him because he was related to some of those people. Upon his arrival at that reservation, he demanded rations for his band, and also continued to raid in Mexico. This was unacceptable to the U.S. government, and many Warm Springs Apaches also were unhappy about Geronimo's arrival. They knew that trouble often came with Geronimo. Indeed, the Warm Springs Apaches soon lost their reservation in the consolidation of Apache reservations. To this day, many descendants blame Geronimo for that, although it was probably inevitable. John Clum, the agent at the San Carlos reservation, was assigned the task—again—of retrieving Geronimo and his band from the Ojo Caliente reservation and moving them to the San Carlos reservation.

NOTES

1. Geronimo, *Geronimo's Story of His Life*, transcribed and edited by S. M. Barrett (New York: Duffield & Co., 1915), http://books.google.com/books?id=AvYaAAAAYAAJ, p. 119.

2. Edwin R. Sweeney, *Mangas Coloradas, Chief of the Chiricahua Apaches* (Norman: University of Oklahoma Press, 1998), p. 447.

3. Sweeney, *Mangas Coloradas*, pp. 448–450.

4. Dan L. Thrapp, *The Conquest of Apacheria* (Norman: University of Oklahoma Press, 1967), pp. 21–22.

5. Lee Myers, "The Enigma of Mangas Coloradas' Death," *New Mexico Historical Review* 41:4 (October 1966): pp. 287–302.

6. Sweeney, *Mangas Coloradas*, pp. 455–457.

7. Myers, "The Enigma of Mangas Coloradas' Death," p. 296.

8. Angie Debo, *Geronimo: The Man, His Time, His Place* (Norman: University of Oklahoma Press, 1976), p. 69.

9. Thrapp, *The Conquest of Apacheria*, p. 22.

10. "Protection Badly Wanted for Arizona," *The Weekly Arizona Miner*, 7:7 (February 12, 1870): p. 2.

11. David Roberts, *Once They Moved Like the Wind: Cochise, Geronimo, and the Apache Wars* (New York: Simon & Schuster, 1993), pp. 73–74.

12. Angie Debo's research shows that Skinya's splinter group was responsible for the incident for which all the Chiricahua Apaches were blamed, and ultimately led to their forced relocation to the San Carlos Agency.

13. Debo, *Geronimo*, pp. 97–98.

14. John Clum, "Geronimo," *New Mexico Historical Review* 3:1 (January 1928): pp. 7–8.

15. John G. Bourke, *On the Border with Crook* (Lincoln: University of Nebraska Press, 1891), pp. 439–440.

16. Clum, "Geronimo," pp. 10–11.

17. Neil B. Carmony, ed., *Apache Days and Tombstone Nights: John Clum's Autobiography, 1877–1887* (Silver City, NM: High-Lonesome Books, 1997), p. 8.

Chapter 5

THE FIRST SURRENDER

CAPTURING GERONIMO

As Arizona began to fill with settlers during the 1870s, and the government sought to concentrate the Apaches on a single reservation to save money and make more land available to settlers, Geronimo's band wasn't the only group who decided to leave San Carlos. There were so many Apaches at San Carlos, it was difficult to keep track of everyone, and many small groups of Apaches left quietly and began to wander through the southwest, always moving in order to avoid capture and return to the reservation. Since they were nomadic, the most logical way for them to survive was through raiding, and the newspapers of the time were filled with accounts of raids; even eastern newspapers reported the news. The *Philadelphia Inquirer* in 1870 reported "According to the Governor's account depredations are continually going on and not a day passes without some one being captured and carried to the mountains by roving bands. If the captive is a man he is tortured for days together, and killed by slow degrees in order that his agony may be of the most intense nature. If a woman falls into the hands of the wretches a fate worse than death awaits her. Herds of cattle are stolen, baggage and mail wagon trains pilfered, and houses burned at frequent intervals."[1] This was fairly typical of the news reporting of the day, which shaped the opinions of the Americans in regards to the American Indians.

Geronimo and other Chiricahua and Nednai bands used the Warm Springs reservation as a refuge of sorts. They journeyed to Mexico to raid, and also preyed on the Papago (Tohono O'odham) Indians in the Tucson, Arizona area. Then Geronimo and his band returned to Warm Springs (Ojo Caliente) to lay low and collect the rations that were due to the American Indians living on the reservation.

This lifestyle eventually came to the attention of the authorities, and in March 1877 John Philip Clum, the San Carlos Indian Agent, received a wire from the Commissioner of Indian Affairs (Smith) with the following instructions: "If practicable, take your Indian police and arrest renegade Indians at Ojo Caliente, New Mexico. Seize stolen horses in their possession; restore property to rightful owners. Remove renegades to San Carlos and hold them in confinement for murder and robbery. Call on military for aid if needed."[2] For Clum, this meant getting Geronimo. His pride was still wounded from when Geronimo had slipped through his grasp the first time, and Clum had since been very vocal about blaming the Apache depredations on Geronimo. He cleverly planned to capture Geronimo through trickery and deceit—the first and only time Geronimo was ever captured by the United States government. The U.S. Army never was able to capture him, although he surrendered to them on several occasions.

Clum embarked on the 400 mile journey to New Mexico on foot, with 40 of his Apache police, and arranged for 60 more Apache police to join him in New Mexico, along with three cavalry companies under General Hatch. Meanwhile, Geronimo's band, numbering approximately 100, was camped about three miles from the agency at Ojo Caliente, and they rode in daily for their rations. After Clum arrived, he positioned his Apache police in the buildings surrounding a large parade ground, and sent word to Geronimo to come in to the agency for a conference. Geronimo later recalled, "The messengers did not say what they wanted with us, but as they seemed friendly, we thought they wanted a council, and rode in to meet the officers. As soon as we arrived in town, soldiers met us, disarmed us, and took us both to headquarters, where we were tried by courtmartial. They asked us only a few questions, then Victoria [Victorio] was released and I was sentenced to the guardhouse. Scouts conducted me to the guardhouse and put me in chains. . . . I was kept a prisoner for four months, during which time I was transferred to San Carlos."[3]

Clum's account of the event reflected his dramatic nature. He related that Geronimo, unsuspecting, had showed up at the agency with the women and children. Clum, who had him surrounded with his Apache police (hidden in the surrounding buildings), accused Geronimo of thievery and murder, and said he was taking him to San Carlos. He reported that Geronimo was defiant and threatened that Clum and his Apache police would become coyote food if they weren't careful. Clum then touched his hat, the signal for the armed Apache police to burst out of hiding with guns raised. Geronimo immediately raised his rifle, as well. During the standoff, Geronimo said he was ready to surrender, but refused to lower his gun. Clum stepped forward to take it from him. He said that Geronimo glared at him with all the ferocity of his hatred, as Clum took the rifle, and the rest of the men gave up their weapons as well.[4] Clum kept Geronimo's rifle as a souvenir, and it was passed down as a family keepsake. Today that rifle resides in the Arizona Historical Society in Tucson.

Later, Clum wrote an article about his capture of Geronimo that was published in the *New Mexico Historical Review* in 1928. After the standoff, Clum recounts,

Thereupon I ordered him to go with the police to the guardhouse. He did not move. Then I added: "You must go now." Like a flash he leaped to his feet. There was a picture I shall never forget. He stood erect as a mountain pine, while every outline of his symmetrical form indicated strength and endurance. His abundant ebon locks draped his ample shoulders, his stern features, his keen piercing eye, and his proud and graceful posture combined to create in him the model of an Apache war-chief. There he stood, Geronimo the renegade, a form commanding admiration, a name and character dreaded by all. His eyes blazed fiercely under the excitement of the moment and his form quivered with suppressed rage. . . . With flashing eyes he permitted himself to indulge in a single swift, defiant glance at his captors. Then his features relaxed and he said calmly, "In-gew" (alright), and thus was accomplished the first and only bona fide capture of Geronimo the renegade.[5]

James Kaywaykla, a Warm Springs Apache, disputes Clum's account in his memoir. "If the melodramatic scene described as Mr. Clum's 'capture of Geronimo' occurred no Apache knew of it, and about five hundred witnessed the event," is his only comment on the event.[6]

Geronimo and the other male leaders were taken to the blacksmith to have shackles forged, and were herded into the corral where they spent the night guarded by the Apache police. Then Geronimo's band and Victorio's Warm Springs Apaches all marched on foot to the San Carlos agency in Arizona, a trip that took 20 days. Once at San Carlos, Geronimo and the other leaders were locked in the guardhouse. By his own account, Geronimo spent approximately four months locked up. He was not aware if he was tried during that time, but reported that he was eventually freed to live at the San Carlos agency.

CLUM GOES TOO FAR

Clum's report of this time showed that hanging Geronimo and the other incarcerated Apaches was planned for the near future.

> My original orders from Washington were to arrest Geronimo and hold him in confinement "for murder and robbery," and I felt that the next step in his career should be a trial in the federal courts . . . It was obvious that the trial and conviction of this renegade in the regular courts of the "paleface" would produce a tremendously beneficial moral effect upon the Indians generally, and inasmuch as Pi-on-se-nay had cheated us out of such an example less than a year previous, I was especially desirous of bringing Geronimo to trial. Accordingly, I advised the sheriff of Pima County [Charlie Shibell] at Tucson that Geronimo was held in the guardhouse at San Carlos in irons subject to his orders or the orders of the court he represented, that he was charged with murder and robbery, and that I was anxious to assist in supplying the evidence necessary to secure a conviction. No action was taken by the sheriff and Geronimo was never brought to trial.[7]

The sheriff never responded, and good old American politics intervened.

Somehow, the military had been ordered to "inspect and manage" the San Carlos reservation and its inhabitants. This infuriated

Clum, and he sent a telegram to the Commissioner of Indian Affairs in Washington DC saying, "If your department will increase my salary sufficiently and equip two companies of Indian police for me, I will volunteer to take care of all Apaches in Arizona, and the troops can be removed."[8] Once the War Department discovered what Clum was trying to do, they objected strongly, and Clum soon found that local public opinion was also against him. One response in *The Weekly Arizona Miner* regarding Clum's proposal states, "What Clum would not do for the purpose of ousting Gen. Krautz is not worth mentioning. The brass and impudence of this young bombast is perfectly ridiculous."[9]

For it was the military that, directly or indirectly, supplied almost everyone's living in the Arizona territory, not to mention the protection afforded to the settlers from the American Indians, imperfect as it was. The truth of the matter was, if the military pulled out, a large percentage of local settlers would leave, since the major economy at that time was supplying goods and services to the military. The local saloons, hotels, shops, and stores in town all existed because of the military, and the various trading posts throughout Arizona catered primarily to the military, or to the American Indians on reservations that the military controlled.

It can be said that John Clum, for all his posturing, drama, and youth, was actually a good agent. He enthusiastically followed the government's policy of consolidating the reservations in Arizona, and cleverly managed some 5,000 Native Americans from multiple bands by establishing an American Indian police and an American Indian court system. He probably did not participate in the now-famous contractor's scam that involved civilian contractors selling inadequate or poor rations to the military for the American Indians and collecting the full amount of money. And his poor opinion of the military, and the belief that he could handle things better and for less waste of taxpayer dollars, may have been correct. However, in spite of his good intentions, youthful enthusiasm, and energy, he really didn't understand the Apaches, and many of the policies he pursued were headed for eventual failure. In spite of his enlightened use of an Apache police and court system, the Apaches still had no input into reservation decisions, and the concentration of rival nomadic bands into a shared small area with the express intention of turning them into farmers was an impossible situation for anyone. But Clum reckoned without the strength of local public opinion, and without the deeply embedded interdependence between the local military and American Indian reservation system. The outcome of all of this was that John Clum quit his job in a fit of anger, and his successor released the incarcerated Geronimo and his friends without comment.

Clum had become the Indian Agent assigned to the San Carlos reservation in 1874 at the age of 22, his only experience being three years in the Signal Service in Santa Fe, New Mexico. Now married and without a job, he decided to become a lawyer and was invited to join a practice in Florence, Arizona a few months later. He quickly became bored, and deduced that the town needed a newspaper, so he purchased the *Arizona Citizen*, a Tucson weekly newspaper, and moved it to Florence, where he began publishing in 1877. This enterprise was not particularly profitable, and Clum returned the *Arizona Citizen* to its birthplace in Tucson the following year and was able to turn it into Arizona's first daily newspaper in 1879. In addition to acting as publisher, Clum was also editor and reporter, and later in life acidly remarked that if Geronimo had been hanged as Clum had proposed, the United States would have ended the Apache Wars in 1877 instead of 1886 and saved millions of dollars (not to mention lives) on one of the most drawn-out, humiliating military campaigns in history. Clum continued to have a colorful life, moving to Tombstone in 1880 to start up the *Tombstone Epitaph* and to later serve as the town's mayor during the famous OK Corral shootout.

As for Geronimo, he realized how close to death he had come after his capture and incarceration by John Clum. In his autobiography, Geronimo related the events that led to his band living on the San Carlos reservation near the agency in a place called Geronimo (which still exists today), and described how uneasy he always felt living there due to ". . . my own unjust imprisonment, which might easily have been death to me."[10] Once there, Geronimo intended to settle down and not fight any more. His people had rations and no longer had to live on the run, hiding all of the time, and constantly putting their lives in danger with each raid. However, he watched the white men's sicknesses kill many people, and soon became disheartened at being confined to one small area. The people grew thin and weak from poor rations, and smallpox and malaria ran through the tribes. The land was too poor to farm, and the men couldn't hunt; they weren't allowed to leave the reservation, and they weren't allowed to have weapons. It was no life for an Apache. Nednai warriors sent by Juh came up to San Carlos to seek recruits. Juh now lived in the Sierra Madre Mountains and the Mexican military couldn't budge him. Geronimo bided his time, gathered weapons and supplies, and sent word back to Juh that he would join him soon.

ESCAPE FROM SAN CARLOS

The Warm Springs Apaches were the first to break out of San Carlos. Victorio battled his way out, taking 323 of his people with him, mostly women and children. They escaped to the mountains near their homeland and sent messages to the military asking for the return of their Ojo Caliente reservation. Still, Geronimo, Naiche, and the Chiricahua Apaches stayed. Chief Naiche, remembering his promise to his dying father, promised to tell Clum if any other bands planned to leave, but he wasn't included in Geronimo's plans. In the confused aftermath of Victorio's escape, Nana, one of Victorio's chief warriors and Geronimo's brother-in-law, left the reservation and headed back to Mescalero. Geronimo continued on at San Carlos, as did his sister (Nana's wife) and nephew, and about 100 of Victorio's people, who didn't want to fight their way out with their leader to be hunted down by soldiers.

Betzinez, another of Geronimo's relatives, told of a time that Geronimo became very drunk on *tizwin*, the traditional Apache alcoholic beverage made from fermented maize (corn). Geronimo lashed out at his nephew, Nana's son, who, crushed under the verbal assault, committed suicide. Sick at heart at this turn of events, Geronimo completed his preparations and escaped from San Carlos on April 4, 1878, taking with him his wife Che-hash-kish and their children Dohn-say and Chappo, as well as his other wife, She-gha. Geronimo, Juh, and approximately 250 people fled quickly, attacked a wagon train for food and ammunition, and fought off the soldiers near Apache Pass to head south into the Sierra Madre Mountains. Geronimo and Juh returned to their lifestyle of raiding and stealing throughout Sonora, Mexico, and selling their ill-gotten goods in the town of Janos.

At the same time, there were several other Apache bands off the reservation in southern Arizona who were also raiding and stealing in order to survive. This was a dangerous time to be a settler in southern Arizona; the Apaches attacked on a regular basis, and the local papers were filled with constant reports of their depredations. Due to Geronimo's notoriety, he was often blamed for raids that were actually carried out by other bands, although there is little doubt that Geronimo's band did their share of raiding—but mostly south of the border.

THE DIVIDED APACHES

The Apaches were divided—not only into different bands that didn't always see eye to eye, also about dealing with the Americans. Some Apaches chose to continue to live on their assigned reservations in order to preserve peace between the Apaches and the Americans. The Apaches living on reservations resented the Apaches who escaped to live freely by preying upon non-Apache people, because they found it difficult to overcome the Americans' fear and hatred of all Apaches.

Many reservation Apaches were in fact employed by the U.S. military as scouts and police, and their tasks included keeping the peace on the reservation and scouting for the U.S. Army when they were given orders to track down and subdue renegade Apaches who had escaped the reservation. Still others acted as interpreters for the U.S. government or trading post whites who interacted with the Apaches, either in Spanish or in English if they happened to know any. Many mixed-blood children of white fathers and Apache mothers, and also white children like Mickey Free, who were stolen in raids and raised in Apache bands, became interpreters. In fact, historians agree that the only reason the U.S. military had any success at all in locating and subduing the renegade Apaches eventually was due to the knowledge and skill of their Apache employees.

Victorio, still on the loose with about 50 seasoned warriors, continued to negotiate for his old reservation, but it was never to be. Soon, out of necessity, Victorio's band began to raid and kill throughout the southwest in a reign of terror that began in 1879. There were other off-reservation bands that also raided to survive, and Geronimo, located with Juh in the Sierra Madres in Mexico, probably also came north from time to time to raid. Wagon trains were captured, ranches were swept of all their livestock, and defenders were killed. Even cavalry units out on patrol were held up by the renegade Apaches and stripped of their horses and weapons, necessitating a weary trudge back to their posts.

Ironically, it was during this time that Geronimo contacted Captain Harry Haskell, General Willcox's aide de camp, and asked to return to the San Carlos reservation. The arrangements were made with little difficulty, and by the end of the year 1879, Geronimo was living peacefully back at San Carlos with his extended family and members of his band, whom he had missed during his time in Mexico.[11] He was living quietly on the reservation while the U.S. Army hunted down and fought Victorio in New Mexico. Both sides suffered losses, and Victorio fled to Tres Castillos, Mexico, where the Mexican army under Colonel Terrazas trapped him. Seventy-eight members of his band were killed and scalped for the bounty in the resulting massacre. Victorio himself died, 68 women and children were sold into slavery, and more than 150 horses, mules, and stock were captured. The Mexican state of Chihuahua had established a bounty on Apache scalps in 1837 at the rate of 100 pesos for a warrior's scalp, 50 pesos for a woman's scalp, and 25 pesos for a child's scalp. As a result, it was always a lucrative endeavor to kill and scalp Apaches in Mexico. Although the Apaches were historically credited with scalp-taking, there is little doubt that this practice began with the Mexicans and Americans who used it as proof for bounty payment. Apache informants never knew Apaches who took scalps due to their abhorrence of dead bodies, which were never willingly handled. Of Victorio's original band, only 17 survivors made their way back to the San Carlos reservation after the massacre.[12]

APACHE GHOST DANCE

During this period of time, an Apache shaman, Noche-del-klinne, became very popular. He claimed to be in contact with the dead ancestors, who lived happily in lush, wooded areas as the Apaches used to live and didn't have to contend with the ever-present white settlers who were taking over Apache lands and driving out the Apaches. All Apaches were invited to dance and pray with him so that his vision would be made manifest, and many gathered at his camp. The dance itself involved men and woman lined up like the spokes of a wheel, stepping slowly. Noche-del-klinne would sprinkle them with tule powder, a sacred substance, and promise that through the dance, the whites would vanish and the dead chiefs would come back to life. Geronimo attended Noche-del-klinne's meetings, which were held off-reservation near Fort Apache, located northeast of San Carlos in the mountains, but declined to dance. Although skeptical, he was impressed with the Dreamer's power, and was won over by him, as were other Apache leaders of different bands.[13]

Other parts of the United States were also experiencing Ghost Dance movements, which began in the 1880s with Wovoka, a Paiute man who claimed he had visions of the ancestors living traditionally in a lush place with plentiful game. The Ghost Dances were pan-Indian spiritual celebrations honoring ancestors and a traditional lifestyle. The dancers wished to live in peace and bring back a time when all was as it used to be, with no white people. The prophets, such as Wovoka and, later, Noche-del-klinne, promised this would happen soon, and dancing would bring the old times back even sooner. Ghost dancing spread like wildfire among the various American Indian tribes in the United States who had been subjugated by whites and were living on reservations.

In 1890, the Ghost Dance spread to the Lakota Sioux and resulted in the Wounded Knee Massacre and the death of Sitting Bull, when the military interpreted the refusal to stop Ghost Dancing as an "Indian uprising." Likewise, the authorities in the sparsely populated southwest became increasingly alarmed as Noche-del-klinne's visions garnered him more and more converts, even among the Apache scouts. Many of the San Carlos Apaches were requesting passes to visit Noche-del-klinne's camp and dance with him for a few weeks before returning to the reservation. Soon, the San Carlos Indian Agent contacted the military to request that Noche-del-klinne be captured or killed. The Indian Agent at the time was Joseph Tiffany, who was infamous for his ring of contractors set up to defraud the Indians. He became alarmed at Noche-del-klinne's popularity among the Apaches and requested Carr's assistance with the prophet when he refused to heed Tiffany's summons.

In response, Colonel Carr sent two Apache scouts to tell Noche-del-klinne to come to him at Fort Apache. At the time, Noche-del-klinne was holding his meetings near Cibecue Creek, 46 miles from the San Carlos Agency. After receiving no response, Carr marched to the area with 117 men, including 23 Apache scouts. They arrived on August 30, 1881. Carr arrested the prophet, who agreed to come along without protest. The Apaches trailed them on the route to Fort Apache, protective of the prophet. When the soldiers stopped to camp for the night, they ordered the Apaches to stay away, as they were crowding the camp. Tensions were high, and the inevitable happened.

Shots were fired, and a gun battle ensued, although no one is sure who fired first. According to Asa Daklugie, Juh's son, both Geronimo and Juh took part in the fight, as they were visiting Noche-del-klinne's camp at that time. Carr ordered the prophet killed, and a soldier shot him, only to be shot in turn by the Apaches. Noche-del-klinne, wounded, crawled to his wife, who was also shot. A civilian finally killed him with an axe to the head as the Apaches and soldiers engaged in a short, deadly skirmish. In an astonishing reversal, the ever-faithful Apache scouts deserted the army and fought with the Apaches that day. This mutiny would never be repeated in the entire history of the Apache scouts.

At the end of the day, seven soldiers and approximately 18 Apaches were dead, and the daring female Apache warrior, Lozen, had made off with 55 army horses and mules. After the army's return, Fort Apache was attacked by Apaches from two sides, several buildings were set on fire, and Colonel Carr's horse was shot from underneath him. Those Apache scouts not killed in the battle were hunted down and court-martialed. Two were sentenced to Alcatraz Island and three were sentenced to hang, even though no one was ever sure that they killed anyone in the battle. A wife of one of the scouts sentenced to hang committed suicide by hanging herself the same day, so that she and her husband could be together in the afterworld. A photograph taken of the three Apache scouts sentenced to hang, guarded by other Apache scouts, their friends, still exists.[14] The ironic thing about this whole tragic incident was that the prophet Noche-del-klinne's message to the Apaches was one of peace; he worked hard to convince them to leave revenge to *Usen* and to forgo killing for prayer. His death martyred him, and gave the Apaches yet another reason to mistrust the White Eyes.

The U.S. military response to the incident was to send in 22 companies of troops under General Willcox; troops called in from New Mexico and California swarmed the San Carlos reservation, which had previously had no military presence. The fear of reprisals created an atmosphere of fear and unease among the Apaches on the San Carlos reservation. The troops moved in closer to the reservation camps, and two frightened White Mountain Apaches went to Geronimo's camp to tell Chief Naiche and Geronimo that the troops were there to attack them. In the face of this news, Naiche, who had stayed on the reservation for the past five years in peace, as he had promised his father, Cochise, threw in his lot with the renegade Geronimo. On September 30, 1881, Naiche, Geronimo, and their band fled the San Carlos reservation under cover of darkness, leaving behind much of their stock.[15]

NOTES

1. "Apache Indians in Arizona," *The Philadelphia Inquirer*, January 8, 1870, p. 3.

2. Sharon S. Magee, *Geronimo! Stories of an American Legend* (Phoenix: Arizona Highways Books, 2002), p. 43.

3. Geronimo, *Geronimo's Story of His Life*, transcribed and edited by S. M. Barrett (New York: Duffield & Co., 1915) http://books.google.com/books?id=AvYaAAAAYAAJ, pp. 131–133.

4. P. Aleshire, *The Fox and the Whirlwind: General George Crook and Geronimo: A Paired Biography* (New York: Wiley, 2000), p. 149.

5. John P. Clum, "Geronimo," *New Mexico Historical Review* 3:1 (January 1928): pp. 33–34.

6. Eve Ball, *In the Days of Victorio: Recollections of a Warm Springs Apache* (Tucson: University of Arizona Press, 1970), p. 50.

7. Neil B. Carmony, ed., *Apache Days and Tombstone Nights: John Clum's Autobiography, 1877–1887* (Silver City, NM: High-Lonesome Books, 1997), p. 133.

8. *The Weekly Arizona Miner* 14:48 (June 29, 1877): p. 2.

9. Ibid.

10. Geronimo, *Geronimo's Story of His Life*, p. 133.

11. Angie Debo, *Geronimo: The Man, His Time, His Place* (Norman: University of Oklahoma Press, 1976), pp. 121–122.

12. Debo, *Geronimo*, p. 124.

13. David Roberts, *Once They Moved Like the Wind: Cochise, Geronimo, and the Apache Wars* (New York: Simon & Schuster, 1993), p. 196.

14. Roberts, *Once They Moved Like the Wind*, pp. 198–200.

15. J. P. Clum. "Geronimo," *New Mexico Historical Review* 3:2 (April 1928): pp. 129–130.

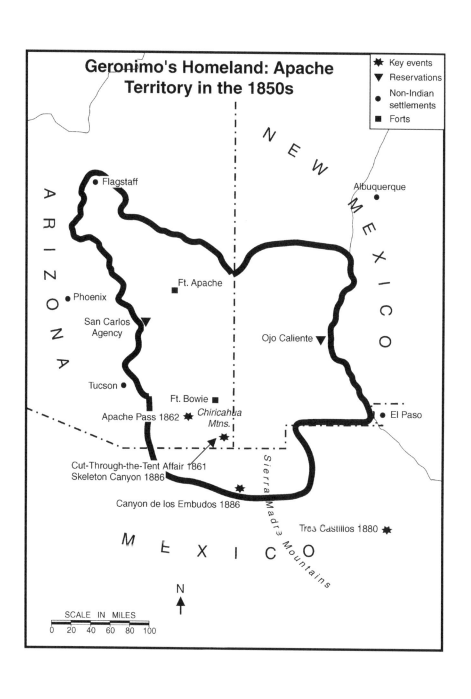

Geronimo's Homeland: Apache Territory in the 1850s

Key events
Reservations
Non-Indian settlements
Forts

NEW MEXICO

ARIZONA

Flagstaff

Albuquerque

Ft. Apache

Phoenix

San Carlos Agency

Ojo Caliente

Tucson

Ft. Bowie

Apache Pass 1862   Chiricahua Mtns.

Cut-Through-the-Tent Affair 1861
Skeleton Canyon 1886

Canyon de los Embudos 1886

El Paso

Sierra Madre Mountains

Tres Castillos 1880

MEXICO

N

SCALE IN MILES
0   20   40   60   80   100

Geronimo posing for his photo, taken by C. S. Fly, prior to his surrender to General Crook on March 27, 1886. Courtesy of Library of Congress, Prints and Photographs Division, LC-USZ62-46637.

Geronimo garbed in his favorite combination of Western and Native clothing. Taken some time prior to his final surrender, it's the face of a man with a few tricks left up his sleeve.

Fort Bowie today consists of rapidly eroding ruins silhouetted against the harsh beauty of southeastern Arizona—the heart of Geronimo's territory. Courtesy of T. H. Marshall, 2008.

Geronimo's band at a rest stop during their train transport to San Antonio, then on to prison. In the first row, Chief Naiche is seated alone in the middle; Geronimo is to his immediate right.

The Apache prisoners became farmers and ranchers in Oklahoma. Here, Geronimo poses in the melon patch with his wife Zi-yeh, his daughter Eva right next to him, his son Fenton, and a granddaughter.

Geronimo gets his photo taken with two unknown gentlemen at the Pan-American Exposition in Buffalo, New York, in 1901. Courtesy of Library of Congress, Frances Benjamin Johnston Collection, LC-USZ62-97682.

Geronimo taking part in a mock buffalo hunt staged as part of a Wild West show near Fort Sill, Oklahoma, where he lived as a prisoner of war. Courtesy of Library of Congress, Prints and Photographs Division, LC-USZ62-127717.

While a prisoner of war in Oklahoma, Geronimo learned how to drive. In this photo, taken in 1904, the top-hatted Geronimo takes a few friends for a spin.

Geronimo as an old man, from a photo taken prior to his death in 1909. Still a prisoner of war, Geronimo proudly wears his U.S. military garb. Courtesy of Library of Congress, National Photo Company Collection, LC-DIG-npcc-19959.

Chapter 6

LIFE ON THE RUN

RESCUING LOCO'S BAND

The Sierra Madres of Mexico, the traditional mountain retreat of Geronimo's Apaches, was changing just as life was changing north of the border, and the mountains were becoming less of a refuge. The Mexican military was getting stronger and more organized, and was dedicated to eliminating the Apaches from Mexico. In 1881, Geronimo and Juh arrived in Mexico with 250 followers, and found themselves constantly on the run, as they were terribly outnumbered by the Mexican military and could not risk a fight they couldn't win. Geronimo came up with an idea to increase the band's numbers: they would return to the San Carlos reservation and "rescue" Loco and his band of Warm Springs Apaches so they could join the others in Mexico. Geronimo, Juh, and Naiche were the leaders of a group of 76 Apaches that set out for San Carlos in April 1882; Nana stayed behind in Mexico to protect the women and children. Even though the U.S. military was warned of their coming, the Apaches had no difficulty getting by them. On the way, two warriors stole two fine horses from a ranch and returned with them to Mexico, intending to catch up and rejoin their party later. Instead, they were captured by the Mexican military and held, their lives forfeit, unless they gave information about Geronimo's return route. They complied, and the results were dire for the Warm Springs Apaches.

Although Geronimo is credited with killing many people, it is difficult to ascertain how much is truth, and how much was manufactured
in order to sell newspapers. There is little doubt that Geronimo's exploits were highly exaggerated, and that many deaths and depredations
attributed to Geronimo were the work of other Apaches. But during
that trip north to San Carlos, Geronimo called a halt at the Stevens
Ranch near Safford, Arizona, and, after ordering the women to prepare
a meal from the sheep and pony he had shot, Geronimo tied up all
the Mexican ranch hands and massacred them. Eyewitness accounts
reported that another Apache, probably Naiche, intervened to prevent
Geronimo from shooting the women and children after the men had
been clubbed and shot to death. That the ranch hands were Mexican
explained Geronimo's cruelty—Geronimo's hatred of the Mexicans
since the massacre of his first family continued unabated throughout
his life. The irony was that the slain foreman, Victoriano Mestas, had
grown up with Geronimo, having been taken captive by him as a young
child. As was the Apache custom, Geronimo had raised the boy and
treated him well until he sold him to an American rancher; therefore,
Mestas didn't fear Geronimo. While they were eating the meal that
had been prepared for them under duress, Geronimo admired Mestas's shirt and asked him to remove it. Clearly the following massacre
was premeditated, as Geronimo left wearing the shirt, which he didn't
want to become soiled while he murdered its wearer. Because there
were several eyewitness accounts to the massacre, there is little doubt
that Geronimo ordered the unnecessary and cold-blooded killing of
the ranch's inhabitants. However, one member of Geronimo's band
pointed out that in later years, leaving a living witness to their deeds
was begging for capture; he maintained that Geronimo's main reason
for killing everyone he met was to avoid capture by the military.

As Geronimo's band approached San Carlos, Geronimo sang four
times to his powers, asking that Loco's band and the soldiers be put into
a deep sleep. Geronimo's party arrived late at night after cutting the
telegraph wires to the agency. As dawn broke, Geronimo and his band
of armed warriors literally kidnapped the band of 300 at gunpoint on
the reservation. The Warm Springs Apaches barely had time to wake
up before they were forced to follow Geronimo. Geronimo's cousin,
Jason Betzinez, one of the Apaches who were kidnapped and who lived

to write about his adventures with Geronimo, recalled that day. "The suddenness of this attack, its surprise effect, and the inhuman order from one of the chiefs calling for the shooting of people of his own blood threw us all into a tremendous flurry of excitement and fear. We did everything they told us to do. We were given no time to look for our horses and round them up but were driven from our village on foot. We weren't allowed to snatch up anything but a handful of clothing and other belongings. There was no chance to eat breakfast."[1] As they left, they were discovered and pursued by Albert Sperling, the chief of the agency's Apache police force, and one of the Apache police. Geronimo's rear guard killed them both and hurried the Warm Springs Apaches along.

They soon took to the mountains, as the Apaches always did while under pursuit. They could move fast, hide well, and locate water sources while in the mountains. Once in the Gila Mountains, they stopped before making a run for the Mexican border. Loco, the Warm Springs Apache band leader, was admitted to the council of elders to help strategize how to move such a large group across the border. With about 100 warriors and 300–400 women and children, this was no easy task. Loco knew he couldn't return to San Carlos; the agency officials there probably thought that his band had gone voluntarily, and were responsible for killing the pursuing police. Since the Warm Springs Apaches needed mounts and food, the area ranchers were terrorized with several raids for horses, and sheep and cattle for slaughter. The Apaches killed at least 50 people in the surrounding area, and the hunt intensified. But at the same time, one of the Apache girls achieved puberty, and a ceremony had to be arranged.

APACHE SUNRISE CEREMONY

The Sunrise Ceremony, a girl's womanhood ceremony, was the most important celebration in the Apache culture. The traditional girl's womanhood ceremony marks a girl's first menses, and she becomes a marriageable woman at the ceremony's conclusion. It is an elaborate ceremony for which the girl must have an older woman as a sponsor to act as her attendant during the entire ceremony. Five deerskins are required to make the traditional ceremonial outfit: two for the blouse, two for the skirt, and one for the high moccasins. Often the ceremonial outfit is prepared in advance by a girl's family, so that there is time to finish the dress with elaborate symbolic decorations representing the sun, moon, rainbows, dwellings, and other natural forces important in a woman's life. The beautiful ceremonial dress is dyed or colored yellow, the color of sacred pollen, and blessed by a shaman. In addition to the sponsor or attendant, a singer is also chosen for the ceremony. It is the singer's task to supervise the creation of the ceremonial lodge, as well as to sing the ritual songs of the ceremony. While the four days of ceremony focus upon the young woman and her ritual passing from girlhood to womanhood, the evenings are social and the community participates. For the evenings, the girl's family must obtain the services of a masked dancer shaman to properly paint and direct the masked dancers. While the masked dancers may bless the area and ward off evil and sickness, their primary purpose in the evenings is to entertain and lead the social dancing.

The ceremony itself consists of four days and nights of ritual, beginning four days after the onset of the girl's menses. It is considered very important for a young woman to have a ceremony, as it ensures her long life. On the morning of the first day, custody of the girl is passed to her attendant, who has the girl wash her hair with yucca suds and dress in her special garments to begin the ceremony. The girl represents, and is referred to, as White Painted Woman, the mother of the Apache culture hero, and a supernatural being representing the feminine and the earth. The singer directs the construction of a special ceremonial lodge, which is erected upon four poles in the shape of a teepee. After the ceremonial structure is finished, the women of the community bring out certain foods to eat, including traditional Apache fare such as boiled meat, mescal, and yucca fruit. After everyone eats, the dwelling is finished, and the young woman finishes her day by kneeling and being painted with pollen by her attendant. A line of people gathers to paint her with pollen and to be painted with pollen by her in return; she is considered to have healing powers during this time. Later, a woven tray containing ritual objects such as bags of pollen, a rattle, grama grass, and an eagle feather is placed away from the dwelling, and the girl runs around it four times, often followed by old men and young boys who pray for long life. This opening ritual ends at about noon on the first day; the rest of the day is social, filled with games, visiting, and food. In the evening, the maiden lights a fire in the dwelling using a fire drill, and outside a huge bonfire is lit.

At night, masked male dancers perform certain dances. These dances are considered dangerous, as the dancers impersonate supernatural beings, and any mistakes can bring sickness or cause evil influence. Dancing at a womanhood ceremony is considered difficult work, but a great honor. The dancers are painted, dressed, and masked by the shaman with great ceremony, and upon their arrival, they worship the fire from the four directions and bless the ceremonial lodge of the maiden. The following dances are of three kinds: free step, short step, and high step. The singer leads the girl to the lodge with an eagle feather, where he quietly sings songs that represent the four stages of a woman's life—girlhood, young womanhood, middle age, and old age—and while the guests are riveted by the dancing displays of the masked dancers outside, the young woman and her attendant resume the ceremony inside the lodge. The singer symbolically sings the girl through a long and successful life as the young woman shuffle dances, dances in place, or kneels on an untanned hide. Outside the structure, the social dancing begins when the masked dancers finish for the evening.

During the following three days, the girl's attendant guides her through the complex ceremony and tells her what to do. There are taboos to observe; the young girl may not bathe; she must use a scratching stick; she must drink through a reed. She is painted with pollen, and participates in ritual walking on designated paths and running to specific destinations. Her actions are restricted and she must eat only certain foods. As a symbolic, living representation of White Painted Woman, she is attributed with healing powers during this time, and people send her their young children and ill to touch. A young woman's participation in a womanhood ceremony emphasizes her role in the tribe as a nurturer and carrier of culture. She participates in ritual giveaways of food and gifts, and stands as a symbol of the people.

The succeeding days follow the pattern of the first day, with the exception of the evening of the fourth day, which marks the end of the ceremony. The festivities on the fourth night continue until dawn, and the restrictions on the masked dancers of not speaking and not being spoken to are lifted. They ask the girl which man she wishes as a partner, and they pull the selected man into the dance ring for her to dance with. The social dancing and feasting goes on all night long, and the final rites take place at sunrise. As the young woman kneels on her hide outside her lodge, a path to the east is cleared, as nothing must come between her and the sun's rays. The singer, using the sacred objects in the woven tray, adorns the girl's head with pollen and paints her body with white clay and red paint, singing traditional sacred songs as he paints. Finally, he ties a piece of abalone or turquoise in the young woman's hair above her forehead. When he is finished, the ceremony participants and onlookers file by to be marked with the leftover paint materials for good luck. The young woman once again performs four ceremonial runs, and at the conclusion of the final run, the ceremonial lodge is pulled down in the prescribed manner, with the poles pointing toward the east. The young woman and her family stay at the site for four more days, and she continues to wear her ceremonial outfit and observe all of the taboos against washing. On the morning of the ninth day, the girl gives a horse to her singer, walking it to him in her ceremonial dress. She returns to camp and her attendant undresses her and washes her in yucca suds, repeating the beginning preparations of the ceremony. The womanhood ceremony is now complete. The girl is now a woman, and may be claimed in marriage. She has completed her ritual training to live in her own teepee and raise her own family.[2]

Obviously, Geronimo's group didn't halt to complete the four day Sunrise Ceremony. But he considered it important enough to have an abbreviated ceremony, even as the group desperately tried to make their way south to the border while under close pursuit. After the men stole enough horses for everyone to ride, the band made an exhausting journey to Steins Peak, located near the Arizona-New Mexico border not far from Fort Bowie, where Colonel Forsyth attacked the band with six companies of cavalry. After a fierce battle, which Forsyth claimed to have won, he left Steins Peak. The next night, Geronimo's band had to cross the wide open San Simon Valley in order to reach the Chiricahua Mountains in far southeastern Arizona, situated on the Mexican border. This was an extremely difficult feat, and one of Geronimo's band later recounted to anthropologist Morris Edward Opler that Geronimo used his power to sing so that the night lasted two hours longer, and they could reach safety in the Chiricahua Mountains.[3] A day later, they had crossed safely into Mexico.

THE MASSACRE

Well aware of international borders, the Apaches relaxed, slowed their pace, and made camp, unaware that Forsyth had ignored the border and continued to pursue them. This time, his cavalry ambushed the Apaches, and the women and children hid in the rocks as the men returned fire. It was something of a standoff, and soon Forsyth's men, tired from the pursuit and low on ammunition, took the Apaches' horses and retreated. Weary themselves, and now without transportation, the Apaches crossed the Janos plains in daylight. The advance guard stopped to rest and smoke, and the Apaches walked straight into the Mexican army. Jason Betzinez described what followed: "Almost immediately, Mexicans were right among us all, shooting down women and children right and left. . . . It was a dreadful, pitiful sight, one that I will never forget. People were falling and bleeding, and dying, on all sides of us. Whole families were slaughtered on the spot, wholly unable to defend themselves."[4] Betzinez and others fled as fast as they could to escape the soldiers and meet at the agreed-upon rendezvous. Geronimo called to his armed warriors and made a stand in a deep arroyo (dry riverbed) with the women and children that were gathered up for protection. Many times the Mexican army charged, but Geronimo's warriors held them off.

Several accounts of the battle tell of heroic actions on the parts of both men and women. At one point, as the Apaches began to run out of ammunition, an old woman dashed out into a hail of gunfire to retrieve a bag of ammunition that was dropped in the initial attack. There are also stories of Fun, Geronimo's bravest warrior and second-in-command, jumping out of the arroyo with bullets between his fingers, to fire and reload lightning-quick, each shot finding a mark, in order to drive back one of the attacks almost single-handedly. Conflicting stories of this battle question Geronimo's courage, which has never come into question in any other context. Some say that he suggested leaving the women and children behind in order for the warriors to escape. One account says that Fun told him he would shoot him if he did. Whatever happened on the battlefield, the warriors stayed and fought all day to repel the attacks of the Mexican army. After nightfall, the surrounding prairie was set on fire, whether by the Mexicans or the Apaches is unclear, and the Apaches used the cover of the smoke to escape to their meeting place. The result of that deadly day was 78 Apaches and 22 Mexicans killed.

Their numbers diminished, Geronimo's weary group finally reached Juh's camp, with few belongings. The Nednais welcomed them and helped them get settled. Even with the devastating losses, it was still the largest group of Apaches ever assembled. After several successful raids to supply their people, they decided to enter the town of Casas Grandes, probably a place where the Apaches were used to trading their stolen goods. Geronimo went along; he enjoyed the bartering and drinking. After trading and getting drunk, the Mexican army attacked in a manner reminiscent of the attack on Geronimo's first family years earlier. All the Apaches scattered, running for their lives; the men fought as they escaped. Twenty Apaches were killed, and thirty-five women and children were taken captive. Geronimo again lost a wife. This time Chee-hash-kish was taken prisoner by the Mexicans.

THE SPLIT

The strain of so many different bands of Apaches living together soon took its toll, and the group separated. Juh and his people returned to the safety of the mountains, and Geronimo, along with his Warm Springs and Chiricahua relatives, stayed on to raid in Sonora, Mexico near the Arizona border. Geronimo had married a young Nednai named Zi-yeh during this time, and she joined the group of approximately 80 Apaches following Geronimo. Geronimo's group continued to raid in Mexico. After the raids they would retreat to live peacefully in the mountains and canyons until necessity forced them to move camp, or raid again. Although they moved around quite a bit, this was actually a good time for Geronimo's people: cattle and pack trains were plentiful enough to raid and to feed the people; there weren't many casualties due to Geronimo's careful leadership and good planning; and they were able to move freely in the land that they knew and loved. As one knowledgeable historian said, "If one did not consider the feelings of the Mexicans, it was an idyllic life, requiring hardihood and caution, filled with adventure but not too much danger, and enlivened by victory dances."[5]

After one successful raid, Geronimo's people established camp at the top of one side of a large canyon and heard drumming from the other side. It was Juh and his people. The two groups merged joyously and stayed together for awhile. Soon the band ran out of supplies and ammunition for their American military-issue rifles; the older Mexican ammunition didn't fit, so a raid to get ammunition was organized for north of the border. The warriors split into two groups; Geronimo's raiding party concentrated on raiding in Sonora for pack trains, horses, and cattle. Chihuahua and Chatto led the party that ventured north of the border, raiding for ammunition. During one raid north of the border, they attacked a charcoal camp near Tombstone, Arizona, and the next day came upon a horse and wagon carrying a family. Federal Judge H. C. and Mrs. McComas were traveling with their six-year-old son, Charlie, by buckboard when they encountered a raiding party near Lordsburg, New Mexico. In typical Apache fashion, the judge and his wife were killed and young Charlie was kidnapped in an incident that became famous. The newspapers picked up on the story and the whole country became consumed for a short time with the mystery of what had happened to little Charlie McComas. Typical newspaper accounts related that he was alive and well and being held for ransom by Geronimo's band, and that Geronimo would only accept ammunition in trade for little Charlie. One newspaper article claimed that Charlie was living with Juh's wife, who refused to release him.[6] While Geronimo's band didn't have the child, the intense and ultimately futile hunt for him affected all the Apaches in the area. The expectation was that little Charlie would be ransomed and returned any day, and the soldiers and traders in constant contact with the Apaches were assured of his good care and survival. He was never found, and there is no proof of what happened to him, although years later some Apache oral histories contain reminiscences about what older relatives said of the incident. The Apaches probably treated Charlie like any child captive, which meant that he was fed, sheltered, and encouraged to become a member of the band. The fact that he wasn't recovered when the band was later brought in by General Crook indicated that something unexpected had happened, which the Apaches were afraid to discuss given all of the intense interest in Charlie McComas. Apache oral histories address Charlie's death; one account relates that he was felled by enemy gunfire during an attack by the Mexican military, a victim of the Apaches' raid-and-run lifestyle.[7] Other possibilities include an unexpected illness or an unforeseen accident as he was adjusting to a hard life he wasn't used to. Betzinez said in his account that little Charlie was killed by an Apache called "Speedy" in retaliation after his mother was shot by General Crook's scouts.[8] All of the oral histories are based on hearsay and agree only on the fact that Charlie McComas didn't survive. Whatever the truth, the Apaches at the time disavowed all knowledge of Charlie McComas.

The other loss to the Apaches from this incident was the warrior Beneactiney, who was killed at the charcoal camp. His closest friend, Tsoe, grieved at his death, decided to leave the band and join the Apaches at San Carlos. Since each Apache was always allowed to choose his own path, Tsoe's friends merely bade him farewell. On his way to San Carlos, Tsoe was willingly "captured" by Lieutenant Davis and taken to San Carlos, where he was encouraged to become a scout for the U.S. Army. This choice was to have serious implications for Geronimo's future. Tsoe, later called Peaches by the White Eyes, became Crook's guide and led him unerringly to Geronimo's camp.

After re-crossing the border, Geronimo's band joined with Juh again. They captured a herd of cattle and drove them back to camp, leaving a large trail. After butchering the cattle and preparing the meat, the women and children relocated while the men prepared a trap for the Mexican military they expected would follow the cattle trail. A troop led by Garcia was ambushed, and although they fought bravely, they had to retreat with many losses. On their way back to camp, Geronimo's power made another appearance, as reported by eyewitness Jason Betzinez. Geronimo suddenly stopped eating and announced that all of the people at their base camp in the mountains, 150 miles away, had been captured by the U.S. military. The warriors didn't question Geronimo's power; they hurried back to find that once again he was absolutely correct.[9] General Crook had returned to the southwest and had come for Geronimo.

ENTER GENERAL CROOK

Geronimo's earlier action of raiding the San Carlos reservation for warriors caused the army to recall General George Crook, whom the Apaches called "the Gray Fox," from his post on the plains where he was fighting the Sioux Indians, and post him back in the southwest in 1883, with the mission to quell the Apaches. Crook's first action was to tour the reservations and speak with the Apaches there; many remembered him from his earlier tour of duty. The Apaches generally seemed to regard General Crook as tough, but fair, although Geronimo disliked Crook intensely and didn't trust him. He was a hard enemy, because the Apaches couldn't run circles around him as they did most of the American military, but he kept his word.

The first thing Crook discovered was the graft and corruption that was rampant in the reservation system. In particular, the San Carlos reservation Indian Agent, Joseph Tiffany, enriched himself by paying private contractors with government money for reservation supplies, including food, blankets, and other necessities. While he received kick-backs for selecting certain suppliers, Tiffany was able to get even more money by reselling the supplies to others, while the Apaches suffered. When the Apaches asked to be allowed to hunt in order to supplement their meager rations, he refused to let them do so, and imprisoned any who were bold enough to ask about the wagonloads of supplies leaving the reservation. Crook took control of the reservations, fired the supply contractors, and threw out the whiskey sellers and traders. One of his investigations established that the scales used to weigh the beef supplies cheated the Apaches out of 1,500 pounds of beef per week.[10] He established a system of Apache-run courts and doubled the number of Apache police, and he instituted policies designed to make the Apaches self-supporting. The White Mountain Apaches were able in one year to raise over two million pounds of corn, beans, potatoes, barley, pumpkins, and melons. Crook said in his 1885 annual report, "I do not wish to be understood as in the least palliating their crimes, but I wish to say a word to stem the torrent of invective and abuse which has almost universally been indulged in against the whole Apache race. This is not strange on the frontier from a certain class of vampires who prey on the misfortunes of their fellow men, and who live best

and easiest in time of Indian troubles. With them peace kills the goose
that lays the golden egg. Greed and avarice on the part of the whites—
in other words the almighty dollar—is at the bottom of nine-tenths
of all our Indian troubles."[11] After improving the reservation system,
Crook turned his attention to the Apaches still living freely off the
reservation. After Crook's improvements, the Apaches on the reservations never raided again, but he anticipated that the renegade Apaches
would eventually raid in the United States, and set patrols at water
holes and arranged for them to accompany pack trains.

Then Crook did something totally unexpected. He traveled down
to Mexico and asked permission from the authorities to enter Mexico
with his armed forces in order to track down Geronimo. His request was
granted; indeed, the Mexican government indicated that they were as-
sembling their own force for the same purpose. Crook quickly marched
deep into the Sierra Madres of Mexico with one of his companies and
more than 100 Apache scouts. The scouts stumbled upon Chatto's and
Bonito's *rancherias* and attacked, killing nine. Crook camped four miles
away, sent food back with the captured children, and said he would wait
three days for the Apaches to communicate with him. By nightfall,
45 Apaches had come to Crook's camp, saying they wished to return
to San Carlos with him.[12] By the time Geronimo's warriors reached
Crook's camp, spurred by Geronimo's vision, Chihuahua's Chiricahuas
had all agreed to return with General Crook, accounting for nearly half
of Geronimo's band.

Crook carefully bluffed, acting unconcerned about whether Geronimo's warriors chose to return with him or not. Geronimo came in to
speak with Crook, who told him firmly that his two choices were to
surrender or go to war. Crook went on to say that he was not afraid
of Geronimo, and that if Geronimo chose war, Crook would eventually win. The truth of the matter was that Crook was running out of
supplies, and Geronimo could have easily overpowered his company if
he had had the support of the whole band. Crook didn't push, letting
the numerous Apache scouts speak for him, and quickly mobilized the
people who were willing to return to Arizona with him and headed
north again. It was the women, who were tired of the hardship of a
constant life on the run, who probably influenced the band to return to
the reservation. In the end, all of the Apache chiefs chose to surrender

to Crook and to bring their people to the San Carlos reservation, with the exception of Juh, who retreated deeper into the mountains. Soon after, Juh tumbled over a canyon into a river and died; his son said that he had probably suffered a heart attack. This marked the end of Juh's diminished band, and the remaining people went to live with other relatives.

However, Geronimo did not return immediately with Crook and Chihuahua's people. He said that his people were scattered, and he needed to gather them up. He said he would follow them to the reservation, arriving a few weeks later than the others. Crook could not afford to wait for Geronimo, as his provisions were gone and his presence in Mexico placed a strain on international relations. The most he could do was to extract a promise from Geronimo that he would voluntarily return to San Carlos after he had gathered his people, although Crook knew that Geronimo could very well change his mind. Crook's return stunned the public, who had given him up for dead, fearing that his Apache scouts had switched allegiances once in Mexico and that the combined Apache forces had wiped out Crook's small troop of soldiers once they penetrated the Apaches' mountain retreat. Crook ignored both the great excitement over his miraculous return and the subsequent debate over whether Crook had captured Geronimo, or Geronimo had captured Crook, and set about trying to finalize Geronimo's return to the reservation.

GERONIMO'S RETURN

Geronimo took several weeks to gather up the remaining 80 or so Chiricahuas, and while he was at it he gathered together 350 head of Mexican cattle to take back to the reservation, as the memories of poor rations and forbidden hunting were still with him from his last stay at San Carlos. He was willing to settle down on the San Carlos reservation, but on his terms. He decided that he would bring the beginnings of a herd so that the Apaches could become cattle ranchers on the reservation. Just as Crook was facing criticism for letting Geronimo get away, the Apache leader crossed the border where Lieutenant Davis, one of Crook's men, met him to escort him back to the reservation. Crook was concerned that Geronimo's people would be attacked by the whites, who hated and feared Geronimo. Geronimo was angry at the escort, since he believed that it showed a lack of trust in his word, which he had given to Crook, that he would return. As if the situation were not delicate enough, Geronimo and Davis were met across the border by persons claiming to be customs officials and who intended to confiscate Geronimo's Mexican cattle. While it's uncertain whether these persons were really customs officials, Geronimo wasn't about to give up his herd without a fight. Lieutenant Davis, desperate to avoid a confrontation, craftily suggested that it would be impossible to move all of the people and cattle through the night without waking customs officials. However, Davis went on, wouldn't it be a great joke for them to wake in the morning to find that everyone had disappeared? This appealed to Geronimo's sense of humor, plus he was assured of keeping his cattle without a fight. While Davis remained behind to protest his ignorance, it was an easy matter for the Apaches, used to life on the run, to gather up all the people and cattle and disappear into the night without a sound.

NOTES

1. Jason Betzinez, *I Fought With Geronimo* with Wilbur Sturtevant Nye (Lincoln: University of Nebraska Press, 1959), p. 56.

2. Morris Edward Opler, *An Apache Life-Way: The Economic, Social, and Religious Institutions of the Chiricahua Indians* (Lincoln: University of Nebraska Press, 1941), pp. 82–134.

3. Opler, *An Apache Life-Way*, p. 216.

4. Betzinez, *I Fought With Geronimo*, p. 72.

5. Angie Debo, *Geronimo: The Man, His Time, His Place* (Norman: University of Oklahoma Press, 1976), pp. 158–159.

6. "Charley M'Comas: Chief Geronimo and Others Declare that the Boy Is Alive and Well. Attempt of Two American to Secure His Ransom Frustrated by the Indians' Fears of Treachery. Further Efforts to Treat Rendered Fruitless Because of Mexican Suspicions of the Americans," *Chicago Daily Tribune*, October 4, 1883.

7. Eve Ball, *Indeh: An Apache Odyssey*, with Nora Henn and Lynda Sanchez (Norman: University of Oklahoma Press, 1980), p. 51.

8. Betzinez, *I Fought With Geronimo*, p. 118.

9. Betzinez, *I Fought With Geronimo*, p. 113.

10. P. Aleshire, *The Fox and the Whirlwind: General George Crook and Geronimo: A Paired Biography* (New York: Wiley, 2000), p. 242.

11. Aleshire, *The Fox and the Whirlwind*, p. 257.

12. Dan L. Thrapp, *The Conquest of Apacheria* (Norman: University of Oklahoma Press, 1967), p. 287.

Chapter 7

THE FINAL SURRENDER

RESERVATION LIFE—AGAIN

Geronimo's plan to set up a cattle ranch on the San Carlos reservation was not to be. General Crook was unable to overlook the introduction of 350 stolen Mexican cattle onto the reservation, and he confiscated them and sold them, sending the resulting funds to Mexico as reparation. Geronimo was outraged, and complained about the incident years later in his autobiography. "I told him that these were not white man's cattle, but belonged to us, for we had taken them from the Mexicans during our wars. I also told him that we did not intend to kill these animals, but that we wished to keep them and raise stock on our range."[1] Although Crook had managed to get the most notorious Apache bands to settle on the reservation once again, this was not a good beginning for Geronimo, and indeed, the time would come when he repeated his past pattern of breaking out of the reservation.

For the moment, though, all was well. After wintering at San Carlos, Geronimo requested that his band be able to live in a different area. Although Crook was unable to grant Geronimo's first choice, the band was given land on Turkey Creek near Fort Apache, further up into the White Mountains. There is no doubt that they found this far preferable to San Carlos, although their request to raise cattle, also endorsed by Crook, was ignored by the government, who issued plows and instructions to plant crops. The subsequent attempts to attach the plows to the wild Indian ponies (for the government issued no stock to pull the plows) provided the Apaches and the garrison soldiers who accompanied them great hilarity. Nonetheless, the Apaches managed to plant their crops and had a satisfying season on Turkey Creek, raising crops, hunting deer, and living comfortably in a traditional manner.

Unfortunately, General Crook had issued two rules that ran counter to the traditional Apache lifestyle. They were forbidden to make *tizwin*, an alcoholic drink, and the men were forbidden to beat their disobedient wives. Geronimo and his people resented this interference in their personal affairs, and trouble soon resulted. Although Crook correctly reported that in 1884, all the Apaches were living at peace on reservations and there were no Indian wars for the first time in years, 1885 saw trouble beginning to brew. Geronimo's people were back at Turkey Creek after their winter at the post, and Lieutenant Davis, who was in charge, was confronted with his first cases of wife beating and *tizwin* drinking. A young woman with a broken arm and a mass of welts and bruises was tended to by an army doctor and Davis had her husband locked up in the Fort Apache jail for two weeks; next Davis gave a similar sentence to a young man who made and drank *tizwin*. The Apache elders demanded the release of these offenders, and Davis refused, so they staged a rebellion by hosting a community *tizwin* party, with all the elders participating. They then challenged Davis as a group, asking him what he planned to do about it.

Davis recognized the seriousness of the situation and wired the general for instructions. But General Crook never received Davis' telegram, and so the entire weekend went by without a reply from Crook. Geronimo became alarmed at the silence and inaction of the officers, having heard rumors of his own imminent arrest and execution by Crook. Some Apache scouts, distinguished by their red headbands, would smile at him and draw their fingers across their throats in a gesture indicating that he would be killed. Mickey Free and Chatto were overheard telling Lieutenant Davis of Geronimo's supposed heinous plans, and some of Geronimo's friends warned him he was about to be arrested and executed. Geronimo finally gathered his people and belongings, and again left the reservation, running for the Mexican border with all the other Chiricahua bands. As they headed for the border, the Apaches killed at least 17 settlers and stole approximately

150 horses.[2] Renegade Apaches again made the headlines; the May 22 1885 *Silver City Enterprise* (Silver City, New Mexico) trumpeted "IN-DIAN DEPREDATIONS: Fifty Bloodthirsty Red Devils, With Their Squaws and Papooses, On The Warpath." According to the article, "News that fifty Indians, under the leadership of that murderous devil Geronimo, had left the reservation on the 18th inst., was received in this city."[3] The settlers were in a panic, and wrote personal letters to the White House, pleading for protection.

ON THE RUN AGAIN

Thanks to the telegraph system that now covered southern Arizona, Crook immediately dispatched 20 troops of cavalry out of five different forts. Along with nearly 200 scouts, at least 2,000 men gave chase to the Chiricahua Apaches. They ranged throughout southern Arizona and southern New Mexico and responded to panicked sightings by the settlers, but never came near the fleeing Apaches, who rode 90 miles without stopping until they had crossed the Mexican border. The only sign left behind of the grueling , relentless trek were the bodies of two dead newborn babies. The American soldiers wouldn't have stood a chance against Geronimo's excellent trailing and wood crafting skills were it not for the Apache scouts, who used their expertise to track the renegades. Crook, moving his headquarters to Fort Bowie, the fort closest to the Mexican border, sent out more soldiers in an attempt to seal the border between Arizona and Mexico. After the border was sealed, he sent two companies of soldiers and scouts into Mexico under Emmet Crawford and Britton Davis. The renegades broke into smaller groups, led by Geronimo, Naiche, Chihuahua, and Mangus (son of Mangas Coloradas), and went their separate ways in Mexico, so as to further confuse and evade the soldiers. One company stumbled on Chihuahua's camp, and the other company of soldiers located Geron-imo's camp. In spite of inflated dispatches describing great victory by the military, the truth was that all of Geronimo's warriors escaped, al-though the soldiers captured the wives and children of the renegades, as well as their food stores and stock. This actually was a great blow to Geronimo and the others, as they depended upon the women for food-gathering and preparation, and doted on their families. Military reports indicated that Geronimo's three wives and five children were captured; only his warrior son Chappo escaped with the men. The military took all of the captured wives and children, including Zi-yeh, She-gha, and Shtsha-she, Geronimo's wives, Zi-yeh's infant son Fenton, an unknown three-year-old girl, and a two-year-old son. There is some confusion about who the other two children might have been, unless Dohn-say (Geronimo's grown daughter) was with them and had a child of her own, which would have been Geronimo's grandchild.[4] Regardless, the captives were brought to Fort Bowie on September 1, 1885, but eventually joined the band members who did not participate in the raid where they camped near Fort Apache under close guard. While at Fort Bowie, Geronimo's two-year-old son died on September 10, probably of dysentery. History tells us that he was very popular with the soldiers living at the garrison, and they grieved his death. In an unusual departure from Apache tradition, the family allowed the soldiers to bury the little boy in the post cemetery, where a small grave marked "Little Robe," the nickname given to him by the soldiers, ranges side by side with the soldiers' graves bearing inscriptions such as "Killed by the Apaches."

Geronimo was able to outmaneuver the best soldiers following hard on his heels with Apache scouts in the lead. For 24 days, his band traveled relentlessly over 500 miles, changing directions numerous times. At the end of this exhausting chase, Lieutenant Davis resigned and decided to manage a ranch in Chihuahua, Mexico.[5] In order to continue on the run, Geronimo's men needed women, so Geronimo and four others soon slipped through Crook's troops on the border to try to recapture their wives, located near the Fort Apache military post. On a daring raid, Geronimo and his men recovered their family members from under the noses of the soldiers who were expecting them, then cut east through New Mexico to confuse the soldiers. Geronimo returned to Mexico with She-gha and her three-year-old daughter, and also stole another young Mescalero Apache woman, Ih-tedda, whom they encountered on their trip back to Mexico and who became his wife. They encountered a group of Mescaleros out gathering piñon nuts, and took the women and children to replace the family members lost by several of their warriors. Geronimo's bold maneuver was followed by an even more daring raid by other warriors, led by Chihuahua's brother Ulzana, as the Chiricahua Apache bands needed once again to stock up on ammunition for their rifles. Ulzana, a former army scout himself, led a dozen warriors on a night attack on Fort Apache itself, killing 12 White Mountain Apache scouts. The warriors then rode 1200 miles over the next two months, killing 38 people and stealing 250 horses and mules along with the ammunition, which they took where they could find it, in an unparalled lightning strike. Lieutenant Davis recalled a conversation during which Geronimo said, "I don't fight Mexicans with cartridges. I fight them with rocks and keep my cartridges to fight the white soldiers."[6] For the Apaches, ammunition was continually scarce and they always made it count. When they camped in the Sierra Madres in Mexico, they were able to dislodge boulders in order to create landslides to take out approaching Mexican army details.

An exasperated General Crook retaliated by once again outfitting a company, this time consisting of 100 Apache scouts, a pack train, and three officers under Captain Crawford, to go into the Mexican Sierra Nevadas and bring back Geronimo and the rest of the Apache renegades. Crawford's scouts marched 48 hours without stopping, and penetrated 150 miles south of the border, farther into Mexico than any military expedition had ever gone. They found Geronimo's *rancheria* deep in the Sierra Madres in an area known as the Devil's Backbone, and attacked at dawn, to find that the warriors had all disappeared again. The Americans were now in possession of Geronimo's defensive stronghold, his stores, and his stock. Not long after, an Apache woman told Crawford that Geronimo wished to speak with him and they agreed to meet the following day at the river below the camp. But before they could meet, Crawford's scouts reported the approach of a large party. Instead of the reinforcements expected by the U.S. Army, Mexican irregulars fired shots, thinking that they had come upon the Apaches. The Americans held their fire and shouted in Spanish; Crawford jumped up on a rock and waved his handkerchief. More shots were fired, an interpreter was wounded, and Crawford was shot in the head. The angry scouts returned the fire, killing all the Mexican officers and wounding more of the irregulars, who finally surrendered and withdrew. According to one eyewitness, Geronimo, who observed the encounter from the safety of a nearby hilltop, found the sight of the Americans fighting the Mexicans very entertaining, although he cancelled his meeting with the Americans and retreated from the combat.[7] Lieutenant Maus, the second in command, took over as Crawford lingered in a coma for days. Maus began the retreat back to the United States when he was again contacted by an emissary from Geronimo, and met with him and his warriors alone and unarmed. Geronimo asked Maus why he had come all this way, and Maus replied that he had come to capture Geronimo and his band.[8] Pleased with the military man's straightforward answer, Geronimo indicated that he was ready to talk surrender terms with Crook. The fact that Crook still had the band's family members, and that he was able to track them even into the depths of the Sierra Madres, proved that nowhere was safe. Geronimo didn't return immediately with Lieutenant Maus; however, he sent nine members of his band back with Maus, with the promise that he would meet with General Crook at Cañon de los Embudos just south of the border in about two months time to talk about surrendering again. Geronimo instructed the military to wait for the smoke signals, then to ride in to the canyon. Lieutenant Maus returned to the United States with the hostages that were surety that Geronimo's word was good; they included old Nana, his wife Nahdoste (Geronimo's sister), and Geronimo's pregnant wife, Ih-tedda. They took up residence at Fort Bowie, as Lieutenant Maus and General Crook prepared for the official surrender of Geronimo.

GERONIMO'S SURRENDER

February 5, 1886 saw Lieutenant Maus again camped about 10 miles south of the Arizona border, waiting for contact to be made with Geronimo. The renegades arrived on time; they made contact on March 15, and, refusing to cross the U.S. border, carefully established a camp in the Cañon de los Embudos. Under Geronimo's direction, the Apaches camped on high ground with the best defensive position, the mountains at their backs and several routes of retreat worked out. Geronimo rode over daily to Maus's camp half a mile away, demanding to know when General Crook would arrive.

In the meantime, Crook planned his approach. Geronimo had seen to it that there was no way for the Americans to effectively capture his band; his mistrust of the Americans guided his actions, and he was prepared for treachery. Crook knew that he would have to talk

Geronimo into surrendering. He brought his usual pack train, some Apache women from the fort to bring news of their families and their treatment there, and a very small military force. He also brought along a Tombstone photographer, C. S. Fly, who asked to be present at the surrender. Fly's presumption as he posed the renegade Apaches, ordering them this way and that, was shocking to the military men who knew well how deadly they could be. However, his photographs of this historic event are revealing to this day in their unique depiction of the renegade Apaches prior to surrender. General Crook also brought his aide, John Bourke, who recorded the meeting verbatim for posterity. Crook decided that he would use his usual tactics of "confidence, bluff, and personal force" to try to divide the Apache leaders, since he felt that others were ready for surrender, but that Geronimo, of his own accord, would not surrender without many conditions that would be too difficult for Crook to meet.[9]

On March 25, 1886, General Crook and his men met with Geronimo at the appointed place. Geronimo began the proceedings by choosing an interpreter from among those brought by Crook and launching into a long explanation about why he had fled Turkey Creek. He said on record that he had fled the reservation because he was convinced he was going to be arrested and hung. He indicated his willingness to return to the reservation and live in peace, but the time had passed for that solution. General Crook told him that he must decide whether to fight or to surrender unconditionally. His terms were that the warriors who surrendered would serve prison time for two years back east, then they could return to Arizona to live after serving their sentences. This was not an attractive proposition to the Apaches, and they asked for some time to think it over.

At about noon on March 27, 1885, Geronimo and the other chiefs, Naiche, Chihuahua, and Nana, who by now was so old he was senile, met with General Crook and surrendered fully. After formal speeches from Chihuahua and Naiche, Geronimo said, "Once I moved about like the wind. Now I surrender to you and that is all. . . . Whatever you tell me is true. We are all satisfied of that. I hope the day may come when my word shall be as strong with you as yours is with me."[10] And with a firm handshake between Geronimo and General Crook, the surrender became final.

THE FINAL SURRENDER IS NOT FINAL

General Crook rode ahead back to Fort Bowie, leaving Lieutenant Maus to bring the Apaches later. The Apaches were not ready to travel, because they were, as Lieutenant Bourke described, "drunk as lords" on whiskey and mescal sold to them illegally by a trader named Charles Frederick Tribolet, an army beef contractor who operated from a ranch just inside the Mexican border.[11] Tribolet and people like him profited greatly from the Indians, and their concern for their own profits outweighed any concerns for the settlers at risk from the renegade Indians, or indeed, for the Indians themselves. Although it is only speculation, it seems likely that Tribolet may have advocated with Geronimo and the other Apaches for the maintenance of a lifestyle of freedom, pointing out the disastrous consequences of becoming American prisoners of war. He was motivated by the impact on his pockets, more likely. One newspaperman on the spot in 1886, Charles Lummis of the *Los Angeles Times*, reported, "Tribolet told me himself that he didn't want the hostiles captured. 'Why,' said he, 'it's money in my pocket to have those fellows out.' And he bragged how much whisky he had sold them and how he had given Geronimo a bottle of champagne."[12]

Though some of the details are muddled, we know that Geronimo feared treachery, and fled once more into Mexico. An officer was detailed to accompany the 76 Apaches who wished to surrender along with the leaders Chihuahua and Nana, back to Fort Bowie. Lieutenant Maus pursued Geronimo, Naiche, and 32 other Apaches back into Mexico, but was unable to locate them.[13]

At about the same time, General Crook received word from President Cleveland that the terms he had offered for the surrender of the Apaches were not acceptable. Crook was told to renegotiate the terms, and to offer the Apaches only their lives in exchange for their surrender. Previously, General Crook had always been honest with the Apaches, and he knew that to change the terms of surrender would result in the mass exodus of the Apaches at Fort Bowie, to the detriment of the settlers of the area. So he said nothing about the terms of the surrender having been nullified, and the Apaches were marched to the train station and put on railroad cars to go east to Fort Marion in Florida. They thought they would be gone for two years, but most were not to return for 27 years, if at all.

Although Geronimo's flight was probably based on suspicions gleaned from rumor and hearsay, his instincts were correct in this instance. A later interview with him revealed that he believed Crook had lied during the negotiations, and he probably would have been glad to hear that he contributed to Crook's demise in Arizona. Geronimo later said, "It was hard for me to believe him at that time. Now I know that what he said was untrue, and I firmly believe that he did issue the orders for me to be put in prison, or to be killed in case I offered resistance."[14] Once word reached Washington of Geronimo's escape, Crook was harshly criticized. His superiors blamed Geronimo's escape on him, and the settlers became completely disenchanted with him. One local newspaper article read, "General Crook, from being regarded as one of the greatest Indian fighters of the day, commanding the respect of the people of the territory, is looked upon now, as I have heard many of the prominent men in the territory say, not only as a monstrous failure, but as a great fraud as well, and is as much despised as he was formerly respected and honored. . ."[15] Crook finally asked to be relieved of his command. He left Arizona in disgrace and was replaced by Brigadier General Nelson A. Miles.

Although his personal policy was to be honest and straightforward with the Apaches, and history regards him as an intelligent, talented, and ethical general, Crook was placed in an awkward position when the surrender terms he was authorized to offer were revoked by the President. Since Geronimo's subsequent escape to Mexico made Crook look incompetent, he was unable to correct the situation, and had to leave.

5,000 AGAINST 18

General Miles requested additional troops; he put 5,000 U.S. soldiers, one-quarter of the entire U.S. military force at that time, into the field to try to capture approximately 18 renegade warriors and their women and children. He had all the water holes and ranches in southern Arizona guarded by the military, and in Mexico, thousands more soldiers were also out hunting for Geronimo. The odds against the Apaches were tremendous. Geronimo recalled in his autobiography that "we were reckless of our lives, because we felt that every man's hand was against us. If we returned to the reservation we would be put in prison and killed; if we stayed in Mexico they would continue to send soldiers to fight us; so we gave no quarter to anyone and asked no favors."[16] Miles dismissed all of the Apache scouts used by General Crook and began his campaign after relieving General Crook of duty on April 12, 1886. Without the Apache scouts, Miles's troops never came close to Geronimo's Apaches. Lummis, the *Los Angeles Times* newspaperman, wrote, "For these two months General Miles has had full control of the Department of Arizona, yet still the renegade has not been expurgated from the Apache page. . . . He has shed more blood in these eight short weeks than in the three years preceding them, and has lost none of his own in the operation."[17] Indeed, the renegades were raiding and killing everyone they encountered, as they realized that they would be killed, if caught. *The Silver City Enterprise* began running advertisements from locals offering $250 for Apaches scalps; one "good citizen" offered $500 for Geronimo, delivered dead or alive.[18]

The citizens' feelings against all the Apaches ran high, and there was continuous pressure to take away what little land they still had. General Miles was unable to recapture Geronimo; in fact, in five months time with all 5,000 troops deployed, not a single Apache had been captured or killed, so he turned his attention to the Apaches on the reservation. They had done nothing but comply with the agents, live peacefully, and raise crops, but still they engendered fear and hatred among the surrounding settlers. Miles decided to deflect attention from his unsuccessful efforts against the renegade Apaches in the field by the simple expedient of removing the nonhostile Warm Springs and Chiricahua Apaches from where they were living peacefully on the reservation. He brought a delegation of leaders, led by Chatto and Kaytennae, both former scouts, to Washington DC in an attempt to get the Warm Springs and Chiricahua Apaches to agree to their own removal, but they remained firm in their desire to stay on the White Mountain reservation in their traditional territory. After Miles committed to remove them anyway, he could find no place that would accept the Apaches. Finally, the bureaucracy somehow changed their status from treaty Indians to prisoners, and they were sent to Fort Marion in Florida to be confined with the other Apache prisoners of war.

While Miles worked on the removal of the peaceful Apaches, he assigned Lieutenant Gatewood to the problem of tracking down Geronimo. Initially unenthusiastic about this assignment, Gatewood changed his mind when Miles promised to make him his aide-de-camp upon the successful completion of his mission. Reversing his decision to use Apache scouts, General Miles carefully selected two Apache scouts that he knew the renegades would respect, Kayitah and Martine, hoping that they could contact Geronimo without being shot, since they were related to some of the renegades. Gatewood added the excellent interpreter George Wratten to his party and set off for Mexico by mule. Word reached the party that Geronimo's band had attempted to make a peace treaty with the Mexicans in return for supplies, as they were worn out from living on the run. The scouts located Geronimo high in the Torres Mountains and urged him to have a talk with Gatewood, saying that the troops were arriving from all directions and intended to kill every one of the renegades if it took 50 years. It was true that Captain Lawton's command was also in the field, with orders to kill rather than negotiate with and capture Geronimo. Gatewood had joined forces with Lawton and had convinced him to let him first attempt to secure Geronimo's surrender, before Lawton carried out his mission. Gatewood's health was suffering from the rigors of the trip, but he pressed forward with his mission to peacefully obtain Geronimo's surrender.

SURRENDER AT LAST

Geronimo agreed to a conference with Gatewood and said that he would only leave the warpath if he and his party could settle down on the reservation at Turkey Creek with their relatives and live as before, with full amnesty. Gatewood's terms were for Geronimo and the renegades to surrender and be transported as prisoners of war to Florida in order to wait the final decision of the President, or to fight to the end. After sharing a meal of army provisions, and breaking out 15 pounds of tobacco and rolling papers, Gatewood broke the news to the Apaches that their relatives no longer lived on the reservation, but had been removed to Florida. As they spoke, President Cleveland was telegraphing the War Department with the message, "I hope nothing will be done with Geronimo which will prevent our treating him as a prisoner of war, if we cannot hang him, which I would much prefer."[19] At the conclusion of this meeting, Geronimo preferred to fight, but he gave Gatewood and his people a safe pass to get back to their camp, where Captain Lawton and the supply train waited.

At some time later, probably the following morning, Geronimo again contacted Gatewood to discuss surrender terms with General Miles. He asked Gatewood questions about what kind of man General Miles was, and whether he could trust him. According to Betzinez's account, it was the other three key warriors with Geronimo who caused his about-face on the issue of surrender. Perico, Fun, and Ahnandia were regarded by Geronimo as not only his lieutenants, but also his close relatives. When they told him that they missed their families and wanted to be with them, he listened to them. Group consensus was the way Apaches made decisions. It was clear that this decision was not Geronimo's choice, but it was also clear that there was no reason for him to go on fighting alone if all his warriors left him. That day they agreed to meet with General Miles in Skeleton Canyon, just 20 miles north of the Mexican border, in order to discuss their surrender. The trip to Skeleton Canyon, with Gatewood's party escorting the Apaches, was fraught with tension, especially when they rested at a watering hole in Guadalupe Canyon where earlier, Geronimo's band had engaged with and killed several men under Lawton's command. Everyone spent a nervous night as some of the younger officers in Lawton's command suggested that the Apaches be murdered then and there, but Gatewood held firm.

Geronimo and his group arrived first at Skeleton Canyon, but General Miles delayed. He remembered well what happened to General Crook, and he wanted to make sure that Geronimo would stay put, and not run off, leaving him to be criticized and ridiculed as Crook had been. He sent messengers to Gatewood, suggesting that he should restrain the Apaches, but there really was no way to do this. Finally, General Miles arrived, and Geronimo surrendered to him formally on September 4, 1886 in Skeleton Canyon. Samuel Kenoi, one Apache who was with Geronimo during the surrender proceedings with General Miles, recalled Geronimo's explanation of his break-out: "The second time I went on the war-path it was because of your having so many Indian secret service men telling you some false story about me. . . . Some of your own white soldiers, when they saw me and some of my men, would motion as though they were going to cut our throats."[20]

In his autobiography, Geronimo related General Miles's promise to reunite the renegades with their families in Florida, which was a key consideration in the Apaches' decision to surrender. Miles further promised, "I will take you under Government protection; I will build you a house; I will fence you much land; I will give you cattle, horses, mules, and farming implements. You will be furnished with men to work the farm, for you yourself will not have to work. In the fall I will send you blankets and clothing so that you will not suffer from cold in the winter time. There is plenty of timber, water, and grass in the land to which I will send you. You will live with your tribe and with your family. If you agree to this treaty you shall see your family within five days."[21] General Miles and Geronimo stood between the troops and the warriors and pledged to live by their treaty as long as the rock placed there should last. Lawton then piled stones to make a 6 foot by 10 foot monument to commemorate the surrender of Geronimo. As they rode together the next day to Fort Bowie, Geronimo remarked, "This is the fourth time I have surrendered." Miles replied, "And I think it is the last time."[22]

General Miles never kept his promises to Geronimo; all of the renegades were immediately taken to Fort Bowie and placed on a train bound for a military prison in Florida. The haste in which Miles shipped the Apaches off to Florida was due partly to the fact that the local civil authorities in both Arizona and New Mexico were requesting that Geronimo be turned over to them to stand trial for murder. Indeed, his own officers needed to restrain some of the soldiers from shooting Geronimo while he was in custody, as the hatred against him ran so high.

NOTES

1. Geronimo, *Geronimo's Story of His Life*, transcribed and edited by S. M. Barrett (New York: Duffield & Co., 1915), http://books.google.com/books?id=AvYaAAAAYAAJ, p. 135.

2. David Roberts, *Once They Moved Like the Wind: Cochise, Geronimo, and the Apache Wars* (New York: Simon & Schuster, 1993), p. 258.

3. W. H. Mullane, *Apache Raids: News about Indian Activity in the Southwest as Reported in the Silver City Enterprise*, November 1882 through August 1886 (n.p.: William H. Mullane, 1968), p. 14.

4. Angie Debo, *Geronimo: The Man, His Time, His Place* (Norman: University of Oklahoma Press, 1976), pp. 244–246.

5. Roberts, *Once They Moved Like the Wind*, p. 262.

6. Britton Davis, *The Truth About Geronimo* (Lincoln: University of Nebraska Press, 1929), p. 172.

7. Debo, *Geronimo*, p. 250.

8. Debo, *Geronimo*, p. 251.

9. P. Aleshire, *The Fox and the Whirlwind: General George Crook and Geronimo: A Paired Biography* (New York: Wiley, 2000), p. 280.

10. Debo, *Geronimo*, p. 262.

11. John G. Bourke, *On The Border With Crook* (Lincoln: University of Nebraska Press, 1891), p. 480.

12. Charles R. Lummis, *General Crook and the Apache Wars*, edited by Turbese Lummis Fiske (Flagstaff: Northland Press, 1966), pp. 16–17.

13. Jay Van Orden, *Geronimo's Surrender: The 1886 C.S. Fly Photographs* (Tucson: Arizona Historical Society, 1991), p. 4.

14. Geronimo, *Geronimo's Story of His Life*, p. 138.

15. Mullane, *Apache Raids*, p. 7.

16. Geronimo, *Geronimo's Story of His Life*, p.141.

17. Lummis, *General Crook and the Apache Wars*, p. 144.

18. Mullane, *Apache Raids*, p.52.

19. Debo, *Geronimo*, p.283.

20. Samuel Kenoi, "A Chiricahua Apache's Account of the Geronimo Campaign of 1886," recorded by Morris Opler in *The Journal of Arizona History* 27: 1 (Spring, 1986): pp. 80–82.

21. Geronimo, *Geronimo's Story of His Life*, pp. 145–146.

22. Debo, *Geronimo*, p. 293.

Chapter 8

A PRISONER'S LIFE

THE TRIP EAST

As soon as the renegades shipped out on trains heading east, General Miles oversaw the removal of the peaceful Apaches. Although he told Geronimo's band that their families were already waiting for them in Florida, the reservation Apaches were the last to be sent east. Chihuahua's band was the first to be sent to Fort Marion in St. Augustine, Florida. Geronimo's renegades shipped out next, although their trip across the country was interrupted in San Antonio.

Another group of Apaches shipped to the Florida prison on the train were the faithful Apache scouts who had helped the U.S. military during the Geronimo campaign. Sam Kenoi, an 11-year-old at the time, was sent to Florida with the other peaceful Chiricahuas living on the San Carlos reservation. In a later interview, he described what had happened: "After all the Indian scouts came home from the expedition, when they thought they were all at home at Fort Apache, they called all the Indian scouts together and lined them up. Then the commander ordered his troops to take their belts and guns away from them. By order of the commander to his soldiers, they herded the scouts in the horse barn and guarded them day and night. They threw them horse blankets to lie on. Soldiers guarded them, the very men they had gone out with before. If they wanted to urinate, the soldiers went with them.

After these Indians had gone through all these hardships for the good of the people of these two states, they did this to them."[1]

While it is understandable that the U.S. military treated the hostile renegades as prisoners of war and confined them in a military prison, it remains shocking that the loyal scouts, who were on the military payroll, and without whom the government would never have been able to find Geronimo, were treated in exactly the same manner. The treaty Apaches, who had given up their lands and were living peacefully on their designated reservation, and who were essentially civilians in the Indian Wars, were also treated shamefully. They had done nothing to cause the government to treat them as prisoners of war, and they had no recourse. They were taken, with only the possessions they could carry, to the nearest train station, which was 100 miles away. Most of them had never seen a train before, and had never left the *Apacheria*. Kenoi described how all of the children scattered and ran, terrified, as the train pulled into the station. Soldiers chased them through the brush and threw them onto the train. They all thought they were going to be killed. The cars were packed too tightly with frightened people, the windows and doors were shut and locked, and soldiers guarded each end of every passenger car. It was hot and airless, with poor sanitary conditions, and a horrible stench pervaded the cars. The trip took a week; finally, the 381 Apaches arrived at Fort Marion on September 20, 1886.

The train containing Geronimo and the renegades commenced its journey to the east coast at about the same time a flurry of telegraphs began between General Miles and the U.S. government regarding the disposition of the band. Initially, General Miles wired General O. O. Howard, Pacific Division commandant, that the Apaches with Geronimo had surrendered unconditionally, which was untrue. Howard relayed this message to Washington and asked for a decision regarding the disposition of the prisoners of war. President Cleveland ordered them held and tried for their crimes, recommending that they be incarcerated in the nearest garrison. By that time the prisoners were en route to Florida on the train. Miles next informed General Howard that his assumption that the Apache renegades had surrendered unconditionally was wrong, that they had surrendered with the understanding they would be exiled. At this point, the Secretary of War ordered the train stopped and the Apaches detained, which resulted in a six-week layover in San Antonio, Texas for Geronimo and his companions. While they languished in San Antonio, the War Department looked for two telegrams that General Miles said he had received; one authorized him to negotiate surrender terms, and the other directed him to send the renegades to Florida. The telegrams were never found (possibly because they never existed), and President Cleveland ordered General Howard to send him a detailed report of Geronimo's capture, a directive with which Howard was unable to comply, as he lacked information about the incident. The War Department then requested a report from General Miles, which he submitted, but which contained no substantive or useful information. Finally, the War Department, in desperation, requested that Geronimo and Naiche be interviewed regarding their terms of surrender. Their stories were consistent, so finally the administration was able to ascertain what had been promised at the time of surrender in violation of presidential orders. At that point, civilian authorities in Arizona and New Mexico intervened, demanding to try Geronimo for his crimes, with the express intent of hanging him and his warriors. President Cleveland had his cabinet consider the disposition of the Apache prisoners of war in two meetings in October 1886, whereupon they decided to separate the renegade warriors from their families and send the men to Fort Pickens and the women and children to Fort Marion.[2] While the administration chose to ignore the promises that Miles made to Geronimo, they felt that they could not hand him over to civil authorities. The final result was expressed in a telegram from President Cleveland: The renegades would be sent to prison at Fort Pickens, also near Pensacola, Florida. An abandoned fortress, Fort Pickens, was located on Santa Rosa Island. It was surrounded by the Atlantic Ocean, and was visible to the prisoners at Fort Marion. Geronimo didn't get his reservation and his cattle ranch, but he did manage to escape once again with his life.

PRISON LIFE IN FLORIDA

At Fort Marion, the peaceful Apache men, women, and children, were imprisoned. It would be 27 years before they would be allowed to return home. The guards gave them meat and bread daily, but due to a lack of available wood they made only small fires in the old dungeon of the prison to cook their meat. There was little to do, and they had to sleep on cement floors. The Apaches were unused to the hot, humid climate, and they died quickly in the crowded prison conditions as diseases such as malaria and dysentery spread.

In his autobiography, Geronimo addressed his years as a captive in Florida briefly and pointedly, saying only "For nearly two years we were kept at hard labor in this place and we did not see our families until May, 1887. This treatment was in direct violation of our treaty made at Skeleton Cañon. . . . We had no property, and I looked in vain for General Miles to send me to that land of which he had spoken; I longed in vain for the implements, house, and stock that General Miles had promised me."[3] Instead, Geronimo and his warriors worked daylong cleaning and repairing the old fortress, after the women and children with their party were sent to Fort Marion to be with the other 400-plus Apaches. Chihuahua's group had already settled into their prison lives at old Fort Marion. The Apaches were described as docile prisoners, and the officer in charge, Loomis Langdon, made several recommendations such as having a well dug for healthy water, which improved conditions. However, his suggestion that the Apaches be relocated as a group to Carlisle, Pennsylvania where the children could be educated at the Indian boarding school and still live with their families, was rejected. The women spent their time cooking light meals and doing beadwork, which was sold to the tourist trade, and the men made bows and arrows that were also sold. Other than that, they had no occupation. They were always terrified that they would be separated from their children. When the additional Apaches arrived, conditions worsened. There was very little room; they lived in army tents pitched on a concrete floor. The two bathtubs issued for a total of 469 people were in constant use. One of Langdon's monthly reports indicated that 76 Apaches had been treated for illness; dysentery and malaria had begun to spread in crowded conditions.[4] Surprisingly, the government cut their rations, and the Apaches became undernourished, which didn't help matters.

During the first year, Geronimo's four-year-old daughter died, but his wife Ih-tedda bore a new baby daughter, Lenna, at Fort Marion. Geronimo was incarcerated in San Antonio at the time. The Interior Department decided that the older children, aged 12–22, should be educated at Carlisle Indian School in Carlisle, Pennsylvania. They asked for volunteers to move to the distant boarding school and got none, so the prisoners were asked to line up and the older children were selected and escorted by soldiers to the trains to be sent to Carlisle. Once there, their hair was cut immediately, and they were dressed in conventional western clothing: trousers and shirts for the boys, and dresses for the girls. They were lined up and assigned names. Daklugie, who became Asa Daklugie, described his impressions of Carlisle: "We'd lost our hair and we'd lost our clothes; with the two we'd lost our identity as Indians. Greater punishment could hardly have been devised. That's what I thought till they marched us into a room and our interpreter ordered us to line up with our backs to a wall. I went to the head of the line because that's where a chief belongs. Then a man went down it. Starting with me he began: "Asa, Benjamin, Charles, Daniel, Eli, Frank." Frank was Mangus's son. So he became Frank Mangus and I became Asa Daklugie. We didn't know till later that they'd even imposed meaningless new names on us, along with the other degradations. I've always hated that name. It was forced on me as though I had been an animal."[5] The worst fears of the Apaches were realized, particularly in the years to come when many of their children died of tuberculosis at Carlisle at alarming rates. When a student began to show signs of the disease, he or she was sent back to the prison camp to die. The soldiers continued to come for the Apache children, and frightened parents hid them; some were hidden under the long skirts of the women to avoid being taken to school. The students lived at the school and boarded out with local farm families in the summer to live and do chores for $5.00 per month, until school began again. Those lucky enough to survive at Carlisle returned to their families years later at Fort Sill as adults, almost unrecognizable to their grieving families, but possessing valuable new skills: the ability to read, write, and speak English.

Although the conditions were amazingly difficult for the Apaches, who had never been confined in such close quarters under such harsh conditions, those who worked with the prisoners said that they rarely complained, and willingly cooperated with the officers in charge except when it came to sending the children away to school. It was the most extreme hardship for them to be separated from their families, and this was undoubtedly the worst aspect of the incarceration of the renegades in the old Pensacola garrison at Fort Pickens. Geronimo used interpreters to write and send a letter to his wives, Ih-tedda and Zi-yeh, his new daughter Lenna (Ih-tedda), and his son Fenton (Zi-yeh) at Fort Marion. Since there was so much public interest in Geronimo, his letter was intercepted and copied, then published in *Frank Leslie's Illustrated Newspaper* on April 9, 1887. "My dear wives, and my son and daughter," it begins. "Are you at Fort Marion? If so, how do you like it there? Have you plenty to eat and do you sleep and drink well? . . . I am very well satisfied here, but if I only had you with me again would be more so. . . . As sure as the trees bud and bloom in the Spring, so sure is my hope of seeing you again. Talking by paper is very good, but when you see one's lips move, and hear their voice, it is much better . . . I hope you think the same of me as I do of you. I think you have influence with the sun, moon and stars . . . Do what is right, no matter how you may suffer. Write to me soon a long letter. Your husband, GERONIMO."[6] Regardless of his demeanor toward others, Geronimo was ever a devoted husband and father.

The Indian Rights Association urged the government to investigate the situation of the inmates held at Fort Marion, and this finally occurred in March 1887. They discovered that of 82 adult males incarcerated there, 65 had been scouts working for the military at the time Geronimo was captured, and 284 of the 365 women and children were families of those scouts.[7] This resulted in a flurry of protest, including a *New York Times* article that accused the government of acting in bad faith toward the scouts it had hired to pursue Geronimo.[8] While the resulting public outrage did nothing to free the friendly Apaches, it did result in a move from Fort Marion, where the Apaches were not only exposed to disease and sustained on pitiful rations, but which had also become a major tourist attraction, much to the delight of the Fort Lauderdale city government.

TRANSFER TO MOUNT VERNON BARRACKS, ALABAMA

On April 27, 1887, all 359 of the Fort Marion prisoners of war were transferred to the Mount Vernon military post in Alabama, north of Mobile. The families of the renegades imprisoned at Fort Pickens were transferred to the fort, joining their husbands and fathers, to the great joy of all concerned. The *New York Times* reported, "Among them are Geronimo's wives and the little girl born to him since his wife's imprisonment at Fort Marion, and who, from the place of her birth and imprisonment, was named 'Marion.'"[9] For whatever reason, history knows her as Lenna. Geronimo's renegades and their families lived a healthy existence at Fort Pickens, with only one death, Geronimo's wife She-gha. She was ill upon her arrival, died September 28, 1887, and was buried in the Barrancas Military Cemetery. On May 13, 1888, the War Department decided to remove Geronimo's party from Fort Pickens to the Mount Vernon Barracks to join the other Apaches. The military post was on 2,160 acres of low-lying swamp land scattered with pine trees and crisscrossed with creeks and bayous near the Mobile River. The land was unsuitable for agriculture and raising stock, so from the beginning there was a problem with a lack of meaningful occupation for the Apaches, who traditionally spent much of their time sustaining their food supply by hunting, gathering, farming and raising stock.

At Mount Vernon Barracks, the Apaches were not confined in a small space, but were initially put to work building log cabins outside the post after first residing in army tents. The post surgeons, one of whom was Dr. Walter Reed, later to become famous for his research on the transmission of Yellow Fever, commented both on the fact that the death rate of the Apaches was high, and that they were debilitated due to a lack of nutrition. Major Sinclair, in charge of the post, sent a report to the War Department decrying the poor rations and describing how the Apaches were selling or pawning their few personal possessions in order to buy additional food.[10] By the end of 1887, the War Department finally began to issue full rations to the Apache prisoners of war, but the deaths continued to mount among the small group. Although the causes and spread of disease were not as clearly understood in the late 1800s as they are today, and the medical reports were sketchy, it looks as though the Apaches succumbed to tuberculosis, and, due to their weakened general condition because of improper nutrition, a number of other diseases including pneumonia also took their toll.

In addition to critical health concerns and poor living conditions, the lack of occupation among the Apaches led to low morale. The Massachusetts Indian Association, a philanthropic ladies organization, raised money to send two teachers to open a school for the children at Mount Vernon. They arrived in February 1889 and were welcomed enthusiastically by Geronimo, who brought the children to school and policed them with a stick in his zeal to have them learn the skills they needed, much as he used to supervise the children's rigorous training in the old days. He used to instruct the children to jump into freezing water each morning, run long distances, and practice shooting with bows and arrows, hiding, and walking soundlessly through the mountain canyons. Now he urged them to attend school, learn their lessons, and behave. Other Apaches welcomed the teachers as well, because they hoped that their presence meant that the children would not be taken away to be schooled.

Geronimo was given a job as a justice of the peace at Mount Vernon, where he was able to adjudicate minor civil cases and assign punishment among the Apaches. This worked well, as it validated Geronimo's traditional role among his people, but he had a lot to learn about assessing justice American-style. He received a salary of $10.50 per month for this duty, and began by handing down harsh punishments, such as six months in the guardhouse for someone discovered drunk, a not uncommon occurrence among the Apaches, and a "crime" for which Geronimo himself was well-known. Another "criminal" received a sentence of 100 years in jail, but by dint of study and practice, Geronimo was soon able to discharge his duties as justice of the peace quite fairly and accurately.[11]

VISITORS FROM THE PAST

The Apaches had other visitors in Alabama. General Howard, Lieutenant Bourke, and General Crook came to visit, report on conditions, and make recommendations for the care and disposition of the Apaches to the War Department. General Howard's son, Lieutenant Howard, reported on the horrifying mortality rate among the Apache prisoners: 89 had died in the various prison camps, and 30 children had died at the Carlisle Indian School; nearly one quarter of the captive population had died in three-and-a-half years.[12] All of the men recommended that the Apaches be moved from Alabama, but struggled with where they should be relocated to. Their beloved Arizona was out of the question, because the feelings against them ran so high among the white populace that their lives would be in danger there. Also, if they decided to go on the lam again in their home territory, the government would never be able to find them. General Crook thought that the Apaches should be moved either to North Carolina near the resident Cherokee Indians or to the Indian Territory (Oklahoma), but recommended the Indian Territory most strongly, as it was more similar to the Apaches' native land. He believed that they should be given their own land on a reservation, and not be kept as prisoners. George Crook died of a heart attack during his advocacy, and the U.S. government, never quite sure what to do with the Apache prisoners, did nothing.

Company I of the U.S. Twelfth Infantry Regiment, the brainchild of Secretary of War Procter, was created in part to alleviate the chronic unemployment problem among the Apache prisoners at Mount Vernon. There were strong incentives for the Apaches to enlist in the Army, such as regular pay, and 46 men from the prison camp enlisted initially in 1891. Much to everyone's surprise, the unit was quite successful, and the Chiricahua Apaches were taught English in addition to army basic training. Company I was given the mission of building a new village on higher ground at Mount Vernon. They finished 75 new houses, a kitchen/mess hall, a hospital, and the company barracks.[13] Geronimo lived in one of the new houses with his wife Zi-yeh, their son Fenton, and their new daughter Eva, born in 1889.

In spite of his acceptance of his captivity, Geronimo took advantage of the government's offer to allow the Mescalero Apaches to return to their homes in 1889. He divorced his Mescalero wife, Ih-tedda, and sent her back to New Mexico with their daughter, Lenna. She protested, saying that she wanted to stay with him, but he insisted. As he related in his autobiography, "We were not healthy in this place, for the climate disagreed with us. So many of our people died that I consented to let one of my wives go to the Mescalero Agency in New Mexico to live. This separation is according to our custom equivalent to what the white people call divorce, and so she married again soon after she got to Mescalero. She also kept our two small children, which she had a right to do. The children, Lenna and Robbie, are still living at Mescalero, New Mexico."[14] Ih-tedda was pregnant when she returned to Mescalero, New Mexico, and Robert Geronimo was born soon after her return. History proved Geronimo's wisdom, as these were the only two of his many children to survive.

The Apache prison camp at Mount Vernon continued to exist, in spite of the government's attempts to disperse the Apaches living there. It was thought that by sending the children to far away boarding schools, such as Hampton (Virginia) and Carlisle (Pennsylvania), and by enlisting the adult males at camp into the military, that the prison camp would eventually disappear by attrition. The children, once graduated, and the enlisted men, when their term of service was finished, were all free to relocate wherever they chose. To the astonishment of the authorities, they returned to their families in the prison camp. In the meantime, reports from 1893–1894 showed the deaths due to tuberculosis continuing among the prisoners.

THE FINAL MOVE TO OKLAHOMA

Throughout the entire time that the Apaches were prisoners of war at the Mount Vernon Barracks, the Indian Rights Association and other Indian activist groups constantly lobbied the government to address the insupportable conditions under which they lived. The Chiricahuas had become an embarrassment to the War Department, which sought to transfer them to the Interior Department as quickly as possible. Even their own fact-finding commissions decried the treatment of the Apache prisoners, and Captain Wotherspoon, the officer in charge of the prisoners at Mount Vernon, issued a report pointing out several more embarrassing facts prior to his transfer from duty. Of the 300 plus Chiricahua prisoners assigned to him, 165 were prisoners of war simply because they had been born into captivity. More than 200 women and children were being held for the crimes of men, and the injustice of holding the Apache scouts had already been exposed by the newspapers.[15] The War Department, which was having difficulty justifying its continued custody of the prisoners, finally came up with a plan of its own, and in 1894 Congress approved a bill to transfer the Apaches to any military reservation. It was the intention of the War Department to distribute the Apaches to various military posts throughout the nation. When General Miles was consulted as head of the Department of the Missouri, which was the eastern portion of the western United States military command, he strongly opposed splitting up the Apaches and suggested that they be settled at Fort Sill, which was in his command.[16] The Apaches were consulted, and expressed an eagerness to move. Several said that they wished to leave as soon as possible, because so many were dying where they were. Plans were made to transport Geronimo's Apaches to Fort Sill, Oklahoma, again by train, and they swiftly prepared to leave Alabama. Ironically, just before their departure, Geronimo's oldest son, Chappo, was sent home from Carlisle to die from tuberculosis, and was buried at Mount Vernon.

The Apaches arrived at Fort Sill on October 4, 1894, a bedraggled group of 296, and built wikiups with army canvas to live in during the winter, since there was no time to build housing. They were welcomed by the Kiowas and Comanches, whose traditional lands they had come to live on. Although they were traditional enemies, the Indians came together as friends, able to communicate in English through the Carlisle graduates among them. The Apaches arrived with nothing, since their belongings were on another train that had been sent to the wrong location and later set on fire in the train yard. The Apaches professed themselves well satisfied with their new location, as they were able to see mountains again, even though they were smaller than those in Arizona, and they could see the sky without climbing a tree. The smell of sage was in the air again, as were coyote cries. This felt a little more like home to them. As time went on, permanent housing was built; the army had two-room houses constructed and the prisoners lived in traditional family groups scattered around the military post. Eight houses were built for Geronimo and his relatives in a cluster near a spring by the post.[17] The military took the lead in having the ground broken and plowed, and oats, corn, and garden patches were planted. At the same time, 580 Hereford cattle were delivered to Fort Sill on August 1, 1895 to form the beginning of the Apache's range cattle industry, something Geronimo had sought to establish long ago on an Arizona reservation, and Geronimo, Chief Naiche, and the others became Oklahoma cowboys.[18]

The military still counted the Apaches twice daily as a means of control. During the long, drawn-out debates about moving the Apache prisoners of war to the west, officials from Arizona still professed fear that they would return. However, the War Department looked forward to ending the Apaches' prisoner of war status and transferring them to the Interior Department. Indeed, the military made no secret that they intended to transfer the Apaches to the Interior Department the following year (1897) after securing additional land from the Kiowas and Comanches to be added to Fort Sill for the benefit of the Apaches. What they did not foresee was the reluctance of the Interior Department to take control of the Apaches, or the difficulties in obtaining the additional land they would need to make the Apaches independent. Although Lieutenant Scott and others expended great efforts to secure the future of the Apaches at Fort Sill, the foot-dragging continued, and the situation didn't change.

The Apaches soon discovered that mesquite trees grew in Oklahoma, and asked for permission to gather the mesquite beans. Lieutenants Scott and Capron were in charge of the prisoners, with the able George Wratten continuing as their interpreter. They were allowed to travel 45 miles to the nearest mesquite grove if they left after noon on Saturday and returned in time to go to work on Monday morning. Taking a few horses, they trotted the 90-mile round trip and gathered 300 bushels of mesquite beans. The prisoners hadn't tasted mesquite beans, which could be ground into a flour, since they had left Arizona.[19]

Since the Army wouldn't pay for their schoolteachers to accompany them to Fort Sill, other arrangements were made for schooling the younger children. They were taken to the nearest Indian boarding school at Anadarko, 33 miles from Fort Sill. This was the one aspect of their move that the Apaches didn't like, but they had no choice but to comply. However, it was not unusual for an Apache parent to trot the 66-mile round trip in a day to bring some treat to a child at school. At least the school was close enough for the parents to visit and assure themselves that the children were all right.

The military assigned a headman to be in charge of each traditional Apache village on the Fort Sill military post. The village headmen were given the salaries and uniforms of enlisted men, even though they were too old to serve. Geronimo, Naiche, and Chihuahua continued on as village headmen. Other leaders, such as the manager of the cattle herd, were mustered into a special scout detachment in 1897 and put on the military payroll. The Apaches raised cattle, planted melons, and baled prairie grass hay. In addition to participating in tribal concerns such as the cattle industry, each Apache man was given a garden plot to cultivate. In their first year in Oklahoma, the Apaches harvested more than 250,000 melons and cantaloupes, some of which they ate and some of which they sold at the military post. The corn they raised fed their own stock, and the excess was also sold to the military. The prairie grass was harvested and baled as livestock feed as well. In 1911, the faithful interpreter George Wratten assisted Martine and Kayitah in petitioning the government for the compensation that was promised to them by General Miles for helping convince Geronimo to surrender. Thus far, their only reward had been imprisonment. They were also enlisted as scouts and put on the payroll with no duties, then forgotten again after three years.

Although the life lived by the prisoners was probably as good as it was going to get, the people still died. Although the doctors finally understood the spread of infection and all precautions were taken, the Apaches continued to die in unprecedented numbers. No one was able to pinpoint a reason for this, although there were many theories. Geronimo explained it by saying that their god, *Usen*, created a home for all peoples. When the people were taken from the home meant for them, they became sick and died. The deaths precipitated more requests by the Apaches to go home, but the government never listened. Geronimo and his band of renegades, and the scouts who hunted him down, all died prisoners of war at Fort Sill, Oklahoma, and were buried in the Apache graveyard there.

NOTES

1. Samuel E. Kenoi, "A Chiricahua Apache's Account of the Geronimo Campaign of 1886," recorded by Morris F. Opler in *The Journal of Arizona History* 27, no. 1 (Spring 1986): pp. 83–84.

2. John Turcheneske, *The Chiricahua Apache Prisoners of War: Fort Sill, 1894–1914* (Niwat: University Press of Colorado, 1997), pp. 12–13.

3. Geronimo, *Geronimo's Story of His Life*, transcribed and edited by S. M. Barrett (New York: Duffield & Co., 1915), http://books.google.com/books?id=AvYaAAAAYAAJ, pp. 177–178.

4. Angie Debo, *Geronimo: The Man, His Time, His Place* (Norman: University of Oklahoma Press, 1976), p. 317.

5. Eve Ball, *Indeh: An Apache Odyssey*, with Nora Henn and Lynda Sanchez (Norman: University of Oklahoma Press, 1980), p. 144.

6. Sharon Magee, "The Many Wives of Geronimo," *Arizona Highways* (March 2000): p. 20.

7. Debo, *Geronimo*, p. 324.

8. "The Apache Scouts in Florida," *New York Times* (April 4, 1887): p. 4.

9. "Indians To Be Removed," *New York Times* (April 27, 1887): p. 1.

10. Debo, *Geronimo*, p. 337.

11. Debo, *Geronimo*, pp. 353–354.

12. Debo, *Geronimo*, p. 344.

13. Turcheneske, *The Chiricahua Apache Prisoners of War*, p. 29.

14. Geronimo, *Geronimo's Story of His Life*, p. 178.

15. Turcheneske, *The Chiricahua Apache Prisoners of War*, p. 31.

16. Debo, *Geronimo*, pp. 358–359.

17. Turcheneske, *The Chiricahua Apache Prisoners of War*, p. 47.

18. Ibid.

19. Debo, *Geronimo*, p. 365.

Chapter 9

CELEBRITY STATUS

THE MAKING OF A LEGEND

Geronimo remained an obscure figure until the brilliant attack he led on the Mexicans following the deaths of his first wife, Alope, his two children, and his mother. A young warrior spurred by the blood lust of revenge for their deaths, he led an unconventional and deadly attack. That incident proved his worth as a warrior, and ensured a name for himself among the Mexican soldiers, who sought divine help in fighting against a warrior who seemed to be everywhere at once.

Although he was never a chief, Geronimo was always a respected warrior, and as he matured, he became a medicine man believed to wield great supernatural power. Power from the gods manifested itself in different ways and in different people; Geronimo was not unique in his abilities as a medicine man. But his power was respected by his people, as were his skills as a medicine man. Not a chief, but most definitely a leader, Geronimo's personal charisma ensured that he became one of the key people that dealt with outsiders, so he gradually became well-known.

As a warrior and raider, Geronimo became infamous through newspaper reports. Although he often observed his treaties with the U.S. military and confined his raiding to Mexico, there were times when he considered himself at war with the United States and raided in this country. Geronimo did what was needed to economically support his people, and when they were on the run, their livelihood was sustained out of necessity by raiding. Geronimo's efficiency and ruthlessness became well known; he never left any live witnesses who could lead the military to him. As more Apache bands were displaced and turned to raiding, the newspapers were filled with accounts of Geronimo personally attacking ranches, farms, and wagons, taking livestock and supplies, and killing the occupants. Some of these accounts were true, but many times Geronimo was credited with attacks by other Apache bands, simply because his was the only personality known to the whites.

MEDIA PORTRAYALS

In the newspapers, Geronimo was depicted as a cold-blooded, murderous savage. The April 25, 1884 *Silver City Enterprise* published this description: "He is described as being six feet tall, well built, weighing 180 pounds, and is about fifty-four years of age, and one of the most desperate and brutal chiefs of the Apache tribe."[1] He was a complicated man, eliciting contradictory descriptions from the various people who came into contact with him. Most of the military men who dealt with him disliked him; Captain Scott, who supervised the Apaches at Fort Sill described Geronimo as "an unlovely character, a cross-grained, mean selfish old curmudgeon, of whom . . . I never heard recounted a kindly or generous deed."[2] General Miles, on the other hand, recorded this description of Geronimo after he met him for the first time at the surrender negotiations in Skeleton Canyon: "He was one of the brightest, most resolute, determined looking men that I have ever encountered. He had the clearest, sharpest, dark eyes I think I have ever seen, unless it was that of General Sherman when he was at the prime of life. Every movement indicated power, energy and determination."[3]

Whether due to his exaggerated exploits or the cult of savagery that the newspapers established to sell their editions, or just the fact that he was the last holdout to battle the encroaching whites for his place on the continent, Geronimo came to embody the ideal of the southwestern Indian and ultimately became famous throughout the United States. When the train carrying the captured Geronimo and his band of renegades stopped in San Antonio, the sightseers flocked to see the most notorious Indian of his time. A San Antonio reporter described Geronimo as "5 foot 8 inches in height and 9,000 feet in meanness."[4] Geronimo and the others were given flowers and candy, were toured around the city, and were gawked at by countless strangers. The citizens of Arizona and New Mexico wanted him hanged, but the people in the rest of the country couldn't get enough of him. Geronimo, ever economically astute, began to capitalize on his celebrity, something he was to continue for the rest of his life. He lived his life knowing that some people wanted to kill him, while others wanted to buy the buttons from his coat. On one day, more than 10,000 people came to see the captive Apaches in San Antonio. Once the Apaches were put back onto the train for Florida, the situation was the same at each stop the train made, with crowds waiting to see the famous Geronimo.

Even after he had lived quietly as a prisoner of war for decades, Geronimo could still make the headlines, striking terror into the populace. One Sunday in Omaha, where he was appearing at the 1898 Exposition, Geronimo had some time off, so he and his fellow Apaches hired a horse and buggy to drive through the countryside. They got lost and were unable to return at the appointed time. They finally found a telephone and someone was sent to bring them back in. Word was out, however, since Geronimo had given interviews telling of his homesickness, and when they arrived back in Omaha, the newspaper headlines that day read, "Geronimo and Nachee Escape—Apache Murderers Thought to Be on Their Way Back to Arizona."[5]

TOURIST TRAP

This celebrity was not lost on the eastern states, and Florida in particular began to campaign to have the captive Indians incarcerated in their territory. Citizens of Pensacola signed a petition to have Geronimo sent to their city. "'The painted demons,'" the petitioners said, would be a "better card than a circus or sea serpent," and give "Pensacola an attraction which will bring her many visitors."[6] Indeed, Geronimo's renegades did make their home on Santa Rosa Island, and tourist boats left Pensacola daily to transport tourists to the island to see Geronimo and intrude in every facet of the daily lives of the captives, who had to live in difficult conditions while on display. One record day had 457 tourists sharing the small island with the prisoners. The captives tried the best they could to turn the situation to their advantage—the men sold handmade bows and arrows to the tourists; the women sold their beautiful and intricate beadwork. Creating crafts for the tourist trade provided employment for the hardworking Apaches and was a way to accumulate cash. The move to Mount Vernon likewise delighted the Alabamians, who predicted that the draw of the Indians would make the area into a popular summer resort. "Apache Village" was also a tourist attraction, although some of the visitors expressed disappointment at the quiet friendliness of the Apaches. The Apaches themselves continued to manufacture goods for the tourist trade in order to supplement their meager military rations. The move to Fort Sill brought the Apaches further west, and the welcome was not unanimous, as some of the citizens had past experience living with unfriendly Indians. It was against the objections of the governments of Arizona and New Mexico that the Apache prisoners of war were moved west. The fear remained that they would break out of Fort Sill and travel back to their homes to continue their raiding and killing lifestyle. In fact, when the Spanish-American War began in 1898, and the soldiers from Fort Sill were called up to active duty with the exception of a small contingent, rumors spread throughout the country that Geronimo planned to go back on the warpath. The power he had to strike terror in peoples' hearts had not diminished. Even the wives of the soldiers remaining at Fort Sill were afraid, and one remembered that the women and children spent their nights in the guardhouse for safety. They anticipated that at any moment, Geronimo would make one last bid for freedom, massacre the remaining soldiers and their families, and head back down to Arizona to resume his original life. As the panic moved up the chain of command, additional relief troops were sent to Fort Sill, and Geronimo and Naiche were questioned about the rumors. Geronimo was indignant at having his loyalty questioned, and pointed out proudly that he wore the uniform of a U.S. soldier. The Apaches' next door neighbors, the Kiowas and Comanches, were also annoyed, saying that they could take care of the Apaches if they caused problems.[7] Still, Geronimo remained a saleable commodity and was much in demand for personal appearances.

PERSONAL APPEARANCES

From September 9 to October 30, 1898, Geronimo and other members of his band appeared in Omaha, Nebraska at the Trans-Mississippi and International Exposition. On the train ride to Omaha, Geronimo cut the buttons off his coat and sold them to the good citizens for 25 cents apiece at each train stop. Little did they know that Geronimo had a pocketful of buttons, which he would carefully sew back on to the coat after he returned to the train. At the exposition, Geronimo did a brisk business selling pictures of himself. Daklugie, Juh's son, went with the Apaches and remembers how the fair's promoters arranged an encounter between Geronimo and General Miles. "Apparently Geronimo had always wanted such a meeting, and this was his chance. It must have been difficult for the old warrior to face his enemy; an enemy who had lied and deceived the Apaches in order to obtain their surrender. They exchanged some bitter words and each taunted the other with being a liar. Miles smiled and freely admitted that he had lied, and then he stated, 'You lied to Mexicans, Americans, and to your own Apaches, for thirty years. White men only lied to you once, and I did it.'"[8] Of course, this statement is not quite true either, since the White Eyes lied numerous times to the Apaches, and Geronimo usually kept his word.

During the summer of 1901, Geronimo was asked to appear at the Pan-American Exposition in Buffalo, New York for $45.00 per month, and he traveled there as well. The following year, the manager of Pawnee Bill's Wild West Show wanted to take Geronimo on tour for seven months. However, Geronimo was still a prisoner, and all requests had to be approved by the War Department. It seems that they approved the requests by non-profit organizations for appearances by Geronimo, but denied the requests by the Wild West Show, Madison Square Garden, and other purely commercial entities to put Geronimo on display. Since Geronimo was located in Oklahoma, requests from the local citizens were honored if at all possible, and Geronimo rode in many Oklahoma parades. Daklugie, Geronimo's nephew, later remarked, "Geronimo was without doubt the most famous Indian in the United States. People flocked to the reservation to see him and to buy something he had made or owned. When he ran out of bows and arrows they would pay outlandish prices for anything—a feather, a hat, or even a button from his coat. When we went somewhere to lead a parade, as we did several times in Oklahoma, he would start with one dollar in his pocket—and a supply of hats and buttons and photographs. Crowds would go to stations to meet the trains, and when we returned Geronimo would have a supply of good clothes and plenty of money."[9]

One of Geronimo's most famous appearances was at the Louisiana Purchase Exposition in St. Louis, Missouri in 1904. Congress appropriated money for the Department of the Interior to create an exhibit showing Indian culture and current Indian education, which created a sensation at the Exposition. Of course, there was a lot of interest in Geronimo, and arrangements were made for him to attend under supervision. At the exposition, the Indian Building contained a model school with American Indian students of all ages and older students demonstrating vocational skills. Also, the building had "old-time" American Indians working at traditional skills such as corn-grinding, pottery-throwing, and bread-making. Geronimo lived in the "Apache Village," a display of native dwellings, and he walked next door each day to the Indian Building, where he had a booth to himself and sold handmade traditional bows and arrows, as well as photographs of himself. He learned how to write his name in capital letters, and charged extra for his autograph. Geronimo even filled the mail orders that came into the exposition. S. M. McCowan, the superintendent of the Chilocco Indian School, organizer of the fair's Indian exhibit, and personally charged with Geronimo's welfare, remarked to one customer, "The old gentleman is pretty high priced, but then he is the only Geronimo."[10] Geronimo always kept his strong feelings for his family to himself, but he must have been pleased to find his grandson, Thomas Dahkeya, and his daughter Lenna, both at the exposition. Thomas came as a representative from Chilocco Indian School, and Lenna came from the Mescalero reservation where she lived with her mother and stepfather. They were able to stay together at the exposition, and soon after the children left, Geronimo also asked to go home. Geronimo had time to enjoy all of the amazing displays and features of the exposition. In his autobiography, he described magicians, glassblowers, a ferris wheel, and a trained bear. "I am glad I went to the Fair. I saw many interesting things and learned much of the white people. They are a very kind and peaceful people." and "I often made as much as two dollars a day, and when I returned I had plenty of money—more than I had ever owned before."[11]

Geronimo returned home to Fort Sill via Chilocco Indian School, where he visited his grandson once again. He was welcome there, as his presence served as a morale boost for the young Apache students. McCowan, who had returned with him, remarked that "he really had endeared himself to whites and Indians alike. With one or two exceptions, when he was not feeling well, he was gentle, kind and courteous. I did not think I could ever speak so kindly of the old fellow whom I have always regarded as an incarnate fiend."[12]

ROOSEVELT'S INAUGURAL PARADE

In 1905 Geronimo was asked to ride in Theodore Roosevelt's inaugural parade, an invitation that he considered a great honor. He was paid the sum of $171.00, and his favorite pony was shipped with him to Washington for the event. When the train stopped at the various stations along the way, he sold his autograph for 50 cents as fast as he could write his name in block print. Geronimo and five other Indians from different tribes were garbed in their finest traditional clothing to ride their horses behind the president along Pennsylvania Avenue. In a sort of before and after civilization demonstration, a unit of Carlisle Indian School cadets marched behind the "wild" Indians in their uniforms. The point was lost, as Geronimo simply stole the show. Daklugie, who attended with Geronimo, remembered the event. "The trip that I enjoyed most was the one we made to Washington for Teddy Roosevelt's inauguration. He was a showman, almost equal to Geronimo. . . . Roosevelt, in an open black car, led the way. He was followed by the band. Then came the Apaches. As Geronimo's *segundo* I rode at his left. Other Apaches followed . . . Our horses were well trained and we put them through their paces. They pranced, stood on their hind feet, and pivoted like those in a circus. Spectators seemed to lose interest in Roosevelt. They left their seats and followed us for blocks along the streets."[13] John Clum's son, Woodworth, was part of the inaugural committee, and he hated to see Geronimo cheered by the thousands of spectators lining the parade route. He later asked President Roosevelt why he had arranged for Geronimo to be in the parade, adding that he was the greatest murderer of the time. In a typical Roosevelt comeback, the president replied, "I wanted to give the people a good show."[14]

If Roosevelt was just using Geronimo for entertainment instead of honoring him, Geronimo in turn had an ulterior motive for agreeing to attend the inaugural parade. On March 9, the opportunity he sought came about as he and the other older warriors met the president of the United States. Geronimo had thought very carefully about this, and had prepared a speech requesting that the Apaches be allowed to return to their homeland, the culmination of his lifelong desire. He began his address to President Theodore Roosevelt using traditional words that honored great chiefs, "Great Father, I look to you as I look to God. When I see your face I think I see the face of the Great Spirit. I come here to pray you to be good to me and my people." He described the history of the Apaches and the whites in this country, and came to his point. "Great Father, other Indians have homes where they can live and be happy. I and my people have no homes. . . . White men are in the country that was my home. I pray you to tell them to go away and let my people go there and be happy." He ended with the plea, "I pray you to cut the ropes and make me free. Let me die in my own country, an old man who has been punished enough and is free."[15] Geronimo spoke through the interpreter, George Wratten, and Roosevelt answered him, saying that he was sorry and had no hard feelings against Geronimo, but that the people of Arizona feared and hated him, and his return would cause more trouble and bloodshed. Although Roosevelt turned him down, Geronimo later continued to take every opportunity to plead with the President for a return to Arizona, at various public forums that he continued to use for his own purposes.

WILD WEST SHOWS

Geronimo did participate in a Wild West show later in 1905. The National Editorial Association was holding its annual meeting in Guthrie, Oklahoma, with the promise of a wild west entertainment to be held at the 101 Ranch run by the Miller Brothers. For whatever reason, Lieutenant Purington at Fort Sill approved Geronimo's appearance, and he certainly received an appearance fee, although we don't know what it was. Sixty-five thousand visitors crowded the grandstands at the 101 Ranch, waiting to see Geronimo shoot a buffalo that had been brought in from a Texas ranch, in a staged "last buffalo hunt." Of course, this scenario exemplified the complete ignorance about the native peoples on the part of the whites who moved west. Geronimo, not being a Plains Indian, had rarely hunted buffalo in his life, and had never hunted buffalo from a moving automobile with a rifle as he did that day! Accounts of the entertainment are sketchy, but the newspapermen were served the buffalo that was shot by Geronimo for lunch, after watching approximately 300 local Ponca Indians ride down into the arena in war gear to surround a wagon train.[16]

CELEBRITY AND EXPLOITATION

Geronimo's notoriety has continued throughout the decades. Even today, his name is recognizable. Modern military units use his name in a nod to his fearlessness as a warrior. There are towns, streets, and buildings named for him in Arizona, in recognition of the name that once struck fear in the hearts of all the settlers who heard it. His feats were remarkable; who else could have single-handedly out-strategized the U.S. Army in its strength of 5,000 soldiers with just a handful of relatives? Once captured, Geronimo had celebrity status; thousands wanted to see in person the Apache who was the object of so many lurid newspaper and magazine accounts.

Geronimo was exploited for what he was, appearing (despite the efforts of his military captors) on exhibit described as "the tiger of the human race" or "the Apache terror."[17] One can only speculate how much more exploited at Wild West shows and sideshows of the time he might have been had he not been an official prisoner of war. It is uncertain whether Geronimo understood this exploitation, but he had his own motives for participating in his own celebrity. Described as proud, even arrogant, and careful of his dress, Geronimo seemed to relish the respect and awe of the public. He disliked intensely the nickname given to him by his Fort Sill captors, "Gerry." He enjoyed the profits from his autographs and his crafts, and he always sought to enrich himself at every opportunity. It was as if he was determined that he should be the one to profit from his exploitation. He was also single-minded in his desire to return with his people to his homeland, and never let an opportunity to voice his requests to those in power pass by. He used his celebrity status as a platform to advocate for the captive Apaches, letting the public know of their living conditions and hopes for the future.

Geronimo became one of the most photographed and painted Indian leaders, and one of the few who had an opportunity to write down his own version of his life. These were the gifts of his long life; his power had told him at a young age that he would never die by bullets, and that he would live a long time. Yet one wonders whether he wouldn't have preferred to die the death of a warrior rather than live as a captive and sideshow attraction.

Geronimo continued to pervade American popular culture long after his death. He is featured in more than 20 movies and television shows from 1912–1994, including *Broken Arrow* shot in 1950. Depictions of Geronimo have found their way into comic books, and in 1943, a U.S. Liberty ship named the SS Geronimo was launched. The 501st Parachute Infantry Regiment selected "Geronimo" as their motto and slogan, yelling his name as they jumped to show their fearlessness—a practice that caught on in the popular culture. For better or worse, the American public continues to be curious about and fascinated by this unique Apache leader.

NOTES

1. W. H. Mullane, *Apache Raids: News about Indian Activity in the South-west as Reported in the Silver City Enterprise*, November 1882 through August 1886 (n.p.: William H. Mullane, 1968), p. 11.

2. Angie Debo, *Geronimo: The Man, His Time, His Place* (Norman: University of Oklahoma Press, 1976), p. 374.

3. Sharon Magee, *Geronimo! Stories of an American Legend* (Phoenix: Arizona Highways Books, 2002), p. 104.

4. Magee, *Geronimo*, pp. 113–114.

5. Debo, *Geronimo*, pp. 406–407.

6. Magee, *Geronimo*, p. 117.

7. Debo, *Geronimo*, p. 377.

8. Eve Ball, *Indeh: An Apache Odyssey,* with Nora Henn and Lynda Sanchez (Norman: University of Oklahoma Press, 1980), p. 175.

9. Ball, *Indeh*, pp. 174–175.

10. Debo, *Geronimo*, p. 412.

11. Geronimo, *Geronimo's Story of His Life*, transcribed and edited by S. M. Barrett (New York: Duffield & Co., 1915), http://books.google.com/books?id=AvYaAAAAYAAJ, p. 205; p. 197.

12. Debo, *Geronimo*, p. 415.

13. Ball, *Indeh*, p. 176.

14. Debo, *Geronimo*, p. 419.

15. Debo, *Geronimo*, pp. 420–421.

16. Debo, *Geronimo*, pp. 423–424.

17. Debo, *Geronimo*, p. 423.

Chapter 10

NO PLACE TO GO

GERONIMO'S CHARACTER

If Geronimo had lived in an earlier time, he would have been an extraordinarily successful war leader and shaman even greater than his legendary grandfather, Mahko. Given his power and his personal charisma, he would have led his people away from danger and toward plenty. He would have succeeded in raids and battles with neighboring tribes. His strong sense of responsibility for caring for his people would have made the band successful in establishing their homes in southern Arizona, and they would have spread to fill the area. Instead, during Geronimo's time, White Eyes from the east poured into the land, and once they found minerals, they never left. The United States, when it added the Gadsden Purchase from Mexico, gained the *Apacheria*. It provided a good route for the stage back east, since there was water along the route, but it was desolate, composed of the Sonoran Desert interspersed with lush green mountain groups now called the Sky Islands. It was also already inhabited by the Apache people, for whom it was the perfect place. The Apaches' lifestyle had evolved over thousands of years to harmonize with the traditional lands they loved so dearly.

Geronimo had a violent, unceasing hatred of the Mexicans, and was successful in keeping them at bay and decimating their northern territories with his raids and killing. Perhaps this could have continued for quite some time, but it was inevitable that Geronimo would either be captured or killed. His refusal to change or adapt any part of his lifestyle, and his casual brutality toward noncombatants marked him from the beginning. Many of the traits that made him successful also led to his downfall. His determination and ability to always provide for his people led him to raid more and more as their on-the-run lifestyle necessitated it. His intelligence and stubbornness and keen strategic sense, which led him to many victories, also convinced him that he could always run and return to fight another day if things didn't go his way. Geronimo led his people to settle on reservations several times, only to flee when things went wrong for him. After awhile, he ran out of chances; he ran out of choices.

While it is a fact that the white people of the time regarded the American Indians as lesser beings, the Apaches had some champions, primarily easterners who had never experienced first-hand an Apache raid. The eastern charitable groups acknowledged the total unfairness of the policy to confine nomadic peoples to a small area and take away the bulk of their land for other peoples' use with little or no compensation, although they still believed in their inherent superiority and right to do so. However, they were more likely to view Geronimo as a freedom fighter for the Apaches, whereas the westerners who came into contact with the Apaches loathed them and feared for their lives, often with good reason. Other Apaches who knew Geronimo and who also wrote firsthand historic accounts witnessed his brutal murders and wrote of them, saying how they hated him when he killed people in cold blood. Some were even brave enough to oppose him during a massacre and save the children. Although the newspaper stories that claimed that Geronimo had in his possession a blanket made of hundreds of white scalps were patently false, there is no doubt that he was capable of casual violence and murder against those he considered his enemies, even if they were women, children, and other innocent noncombatants. Another incident reported in print seems to be true. "He remembered one time when he had gone into the house of the enemy, having already killed many of the people there. Inside, he found a baby in its bed. He had picked up that baby, playing with him for a moment until the baby was laughing in the way babies do. Then, as if moved by the hands of something else,

Geronimo had taken out his long knife, and tossed the baby into the air, and caught the baby on the blade of his knife."[1] This was a specific memory of an attack on white settlers in their homes, and shows why the settlers lived in terror of the Apaches.

Based on other memoirs by Apaches who lived during Geronimo's time, it's clear that there was no consensus about Geronimo even among his own people. Many admired his intelligence, his dislike and mistrust of whites, and his strategic acumen. His strong sense of responsibility toward those dependent upon him and his ability and willingness to always provide food, shelter, and care to his relatives were traits that led others to trust and follow him. Some people viewed him as a warrior defending homeland from foreign invaders. Others, such as the Apache scouts and their families, blamed him for their captivity and their exile from Arizona.

Geronimo was a complex person. Like many of us, he had the infinite capacity to love his own family and children, yet was able to objectify and brutalize others. He looked out for himself and his family economically. He respected some of his enemies, able to admire their skill without liking them. The culture of the whites amazed him, and he valued its technological advances (particularly the rifle), but he never really understood white people. Towards the end, what he understood most about the whites was that they had more power than he.

IN HIS OWN WORDS

As Geronimo aged on the Fort Sill reservation, he made the most of his celebrity, but he never stopped trying to get his people moved back to Arizona. Indeed, when Stephen Melvil Barrett, the Superintendent of Schools in nearby Lawton, Oklahoma, asked if he could publish some of his conversations with Geronimo, the old man urged him to get permission from the military, and said that he would tell his life story for a price. Doubtless Geronimo was already planning the last chapter of his autobiography, which is indeed a plea for the return of the Apaches to their native Arizona. However, Lieutenant Purington, then in charge of Fort Sill, denied Mr. Barrett's request. Barrett then sent a letter to President Roosevelt requesting that Geronimo be allowed to tell his story. Roosevelt, perhaps recalling that he had been forced to turn down Geronimo's request to be returned to his homeland when they met previously, instantly gave his approval to Barrett. Enlisting the services of Asa Daklugie, Juh's son who remained close to Geronimo, as interpreter, Barrett began to visit Geronimo to write down the story of his life. During 1905–1906, Mr. Barrett met with Geronimo and his interpreter, and Geronimo said what he wanted to say, imperiously ordered Barrett and Daklugie to "write what I have spoken," and left. He refused to have a stenographer present and didn't want to answer questions. Daklugie recalls conversations with Geronimo regarding the work on the autobiography with Barrett. Geronimo was fearful and suspicious of Barrett's offer and thought that it was possible that he was a spy for the army, trying to get him to admit to damaging information so that he could be executed. Daklugie was surprised when Geronimo agreed to talk to Barrett and have his words recorded in a book, but he trusted the old man's power to keep them out of trouble. "Geronimo was very careful in what he told Barrett; and I was just as careful in interpreting. Barrett didn't write shorthand; he took notes. He couldn't write as fast as I talked, so he had to depend on his memory for part of what I told him. . . . Yes, Geronimo knew much that he didn't include."[2] Even so, the old man grew weary of the ongoing hard work of completing the autobiography, and probably would have given up if not for Barrett's insistence upon finishing, and his compensation to Geronimo for his work.

There have always been problems of accuracy in autobiographies told through interpretation, particularly when the author doesn't understand the cultural background of the subject, such as with Barrett and Geronimo. While Barrett tried, and for the most part, succeeded, in setting down Geronimo's story just as he told it, there are some obvious inaccuracies that have crept into the account, including one part where it says that Geronimo became his band's chief. Geronimo was never chief, but was the power behind the throne, so to speak; indeed, Chief Naiche shared his prisoner-of-war status all the way through to Fort Sill. Nonetheless, most of the account is quite accurate and reflective of Geronimo's point of view of this time in history, thanks to the fact that Geronimo's interpreter came from the same cultural background, and Barrett's original intention was to represent Geronimo's viewpoint. It is an unhoped for glimpse into one of the great American

Indian leaders of the time. For so many other American Indians of that era, we have only newspaper articles and the diaries and memoirs of their enemies and the soldiers who fought them, which are valuable and interesting accounts but can never give us the insight or point of view of a first-hand account. For that reason alone, Geronimo's account is precious and unusual, and we owe Mr. Barrett a debt of gratitude for his persistence in writing the autobiography to the best of his ability and for getting it published.

After the book was finished, Mr. Barrett again had to pass it by the War Department, which objected to some of the information stated therein. This, of course, is not surprising; it stands to reason that Geronimo's point of view differed quite markedly from that of the United States War Department. The autobiography was finally published with the War Department's objections noted, prior to Geronimo's death. Although he ranges freely over his life in the account, which is not organized chronologically but rather by the topics he wanted to address, Geronimo deliberately left out much, including details of his battles with the military. At the time, he was still a military prisoner of war, and was bitter about his treatment, so the account was certainly not a tell-all book. First published in 1906, Geronimo's biography remains in print, and is also available online in digital format at http://www.let.rug.nl/usa/B/geronimo/geronixx.htm.

Geronimo succeeded in pleading his case in print when his autobiography was published, which was probably his primary purpose for agreeing to do the book. The last chapter of the book, entitled "Hopes for the Future," begins, "I am thankful that the President of the United States has given me permission to tell my story. I hope that he and those in authority under him will read my story and judge whether my people have been rightly treated." He goes on to say, "In the treaty with General Miles we agreed to go to a place outside Arizona and learn to live as the white people do. I think that my people are now capable of living in accordance with the laws of the United States, and we would, of course, like to have the liberty to return to that land which is ours by divine right." He concludes, "Could I but see this accomplished, I think I could forget all the wrongs that I have ever received, and die a contented and happy old man. . . . If this cannot be done during my lifetime—if I must die in bondage—I hope that the remnant of the

Apache tribe may, when I am gone, be granted the one privilege which they request—to return to Arizona."[3]

OLD MAN GERONIMO

A painter, Elbridge Ayer Burbank, was commissioned by the Field Museum in Chicago to paint Geronimo's portrait. He ended up painting Geronimo's portrait a total of seven times, beginning his association with the old man at Fort Sill in 1897 when they met and became friends. Burbank describes Geronimo's life at Fort Sill, including his many money-making schemes (Burbank was, of course, charged by Geronimo for each sitting). He indicates that Geronimo was quite a gambler. "The popular game was monte. Geronimo was always in the game up to his neck. It was fun to watch him handle the cards. He was as expert as the best of them. At times he would get excited and yell at the top of his voice. . . . As we were leaving for home, a white man approached Geronimo and proposed that they race horses . . . That horse race demonstrated the old Apache's sporting instincts. He was ready to bet on anything. They marked off the distance, placed the stakes in a handkerchief at the end of the course where the winner could grab it, and the horses were off. It was a close race, which Geronimo's horse won. The old Indian went home as happy as a small boy after the circus."[4] Geronimo also continued to enjoy drinking alcohol, even though it was forbidden at Fort Sill.

Burbank described Geronimo as a kindly old man, who did the housework for his sick wife, trained his horse to come to him with a whistle, and never left the house until he had put out a saucer of milk for the cat. He also doted on his daughter, Eva, and indulged her with anything she wanted from the trader's store.[5] One day when Burbank and Geronimo were together, Geronimo declared that no human being could kill him, and pulled off his shirt. "I was dumfounded to see the number of bullet holes in his body . . . I had never heard of anyone living with at least fifty bullet wounds on his body. Geronimo had that many scars." Some of the healed bullet holes made deep indentations in his skin, and the old showman placed large pebbles in his scars while making a noise like a gun.[6]

Norman S. Wood, the author, also met Geronimo as he was gathering information about Indian chiefs for a book in 1905. Wood says he was expecting to see a mean, twisted old Indian with twitchy fingers.

"But instead I saw a smiling, well-kept, well-dressed Indian about five feet nine inches tall, with square shoulders and deep chest. . . . He was dressed in a well-fitting blue cloth suit of citizen's clothes."[7] Wood noticed that Geronimo understood English well, but spoke little. Geronimo still used an interpreter, in this case George Wratten, to answer the author's questions about his life and times for the book.

WHITE MAN'S GOD

The Apache Mission of the Reformed Church of America established a church and school at Fort Sill, with permission from the Apaches, after the military had not allowed them on Fort Sill grounds until 1899. "I, Geronimo, and these others are now too old to travel your Jesus road. But our children are young and I and my brothers will be glad to have the children taught about the white man's God."[8] Geronimo led the group in welcoming the mission; as a purely practical matter it was preferable to have the younger children educated at Fort Sill rather than send them away to boarding school. Eventually, the mission built a schoolhouse, church, teachers' home, and orphanage at Fort Sill. Chihuahua and Naiche became devout Christians, and were joined by many others, including Carlisle school graduates such as Jason Betzinez and James Kaywaykla. Asa Daklugie, willful and trained from youth to succeed Geronimo, clung to the old ways, but Ramona Chihuahua, Chihuahua's daughter who later married Daklugie, became a lifelong Christian as well.

Geronimo held back; he was convinced the old ways were best, and indeed, was a practitioner while he was at Fort Sill, assisting his people with traditional ceremonies when he was asked. Still, he began to take a serious look at Christianity. He regarded it also as a source of power, and the whites had proven more powerful than the Apaches, so it was a religion he respected. Also, as he aged and watched the loved ones around him die, he began to wonder about the worth of his own power, which had promised he would not die by bullets and live long, when everyone he loved was dying. He was living at this time with his wife Zi-yeh, whose health was beginning to deteriorate, and their daughter, his last child, Eva, born in 1889. Geronimo's great love and affection for Eva were evident to all. He was also exceptionally close to Thomas, his daughter Dohn-say's son, who lived at boarding school.

In 1902, Geronimo committed to "the Jesus road" in an enthusiastic speech during a camp meeting. The missionaries encouraged his newfound devotion, but didn't admit him yet as a full church member, indicating that he needed to work on his humility and his tendency to drink alcohol. The following year (1903), Geronimo, injured from a fall from his horse, attended another church meeting at which he declared himself unequivocally. He stated that he was old, broken, and without friends. He said that he was full of sin and that he saw that Christianity had the right way to get the sin out of his heart, and he wanted to take that right road until he died. Geronimo's emotional declaration won him membership in the church, and he was baptized a week later, with great ceremony and joy.

However, he saw no reason to discard his old beliefs, and during 1905, he celebrated Eva's womanhood ceremony in the traditional way as she turned 16. Geronimo sponsored an elaborate celebration with Ramona Daklugie as Eva's sponsor. At a beautiful site on Medicine Bluff Creek near Naiche's village, the lodge was erected under Naiche's direction as singer, and Geronimo himself directed the dancers for the event, with the assistance of another medicine man. It appears that Geronimo simply added Christianity to his spiritual repertoire, seeing no conflict between his traditional beliefs and "the Jesus road," which he enthusiastically endorsed. He spoke thoughtfully about religion in his autobiography, "Since my life as a prisoner has begun I have heard the teachings of the white man's religion, and in many respects believe it to be better than the religion of my fathers. However, I have always prayed, and I believe that the Almighty has always protected me . . . I have advised all of my people who are not Christians, to study that religion, because it seems to me the best religion in enabling one to live right."[9] Clearly Geronimo had given thought to spirituality and religion, and he respected and valued Christianity. He also had a great commitment to his traditional belief system. His views about religion were conflicted throughout his life, and it seems that his resolution was an uneasy acceptance and combination of both beliefs.

GERONIMO'S END

As time went on, Geronimo fell back into his old habits of drinking alcohol, horse racing, and gambling, which he had always enjoyed. His church membership was suspended, probably around 1907, because of his refusal to give up these pleasures. Geronimo felt that the church's rules were too strict, and happily returned to his traditional beliefs. By this time, Geronimo had experienced more than his share of losses. His wife Zi-yeh died in 1904. He remarried an Apache widow named Sousche or Mrs. Mary Loto the following year, but they separated almost immediately, and Geronimo devoted himself to raising his beloved daughter Eva. In 1907, he married a final time. His ninth wife, known as Sunsetso or Azul, stayed with him and cared for him during his final days. In 1908, his cherished grandson, Thomas Dahkeya, died at the age of 18 at the Chilocco boarding school where he lived. This was a huge blow to Geronimo. He was never close to his son and daughter, Robert and Lenna, whom he had fathered with Ih-tedda, since they were raised on the Mescalero Apache reservation. Eva and Thomas were his life.

When Eva also began to show signs of tuberculosis, Geronimo despaired. Always before, he was the shaman others turned to in order to discover the source of problems and find the answers. This time, Geronimo asked Lot Eyelash to perform an Apache ceremony to discover the source of the evil influence destroying his family. At the ceremony, Lot Eyelash announced that Geronimo himself was destroying his family so that he could continue to live.[10] While Geronimo knew this to be untrue, it began more rumors about his power, and he again began to consider Christianity since his own traditions seemed to have let him down so badly. During February 1909, Geronimo rode into Lawton to sell his bows and arrows. While there, he asked Eugene Chihuahua to get him some whiskey. In an interview, Chihuahua blamed himself for Geronimo's death. "I feel that I am responsible for the death of Geronimo. It wasn't intentional; and if I had refused his request somebody else might have bought the whiskey that caused it. But I didn't refuse."[11] Chihuahua asked a fellow soldier to obtain the whiskey, then he rode out of town and met Geronimo at Cache Creek, where they drank the whiskey and slept, covered only by their saddle blankets. They woke in a cold drizzle, and Geronimo was coughing and said he'd been sick all night. Chihuahua saddled the horses and took Geronimo to the hospital, where he was diagnosed with pneumonia. Chihuahua, Daklugie, and his wife stayed with him continuously in the hospital until his death three days later. Daklugie said that Geronimo spoke of the past and of his regrets that he had surrendered, and his desire to have ended his life on the warpath fighting his enemies. He also asked Daklugie to take care of his precious daughter Eva. Daklugie was holding his hand when he died.[12] Other accounts say that Geronimo fell off his horse after Chihuahua bought him the whiskey, that he was discovered on the ground the next morning, and that on his deathbed, Geronimo once again regretted that he had not become a Christian, again reliving the conflict between his beliefs.[13] His daughter Eva and his son Robert, both at Chilocco Boarding School, were sent for, but arrived after his death. He died on February 17, 1909, and was buried in the Fort Sill Apache Cemetery with many of his family and friends. Daklugie related that there was always a guard at Geronimo's gravesite during the first few months after his death. Because of Geronimo's notoriety, they feared that his grave would be robbed of all the valuables buried with him to accompany him to the next life, and the memories of what happened to Mangas Coloradas gave rise to deeper fears.

Geronimo's celebrity didn't stop with his death. A long obituary was published in the *New York Times* the following day, entitled "Old Apache Chief Geronimo Is Dead." The article contained a number of factual errors about Geronimo's life, and exhibited the type of sensational language newspapers used when writing about American Indians. It read, in part, "As the leader of the warring Apaches of the Southwestern territories in pioneer days, Geronimo gained a reputation for cruelty and cunning never surpassed by that of any other American Indian chief. For more than twenty years he and his men were the terror of the country, always leaving a trail of bloodshed and devastation." It went on to detail Geronimo's capture and confinement, and contained a quote from General Miles: "Every one at Washington had now become convinced that there was no good in the old chief, and he was, in fact, one of the lowest and most cruel of the savages of the American continent."[14]

GERONIMO LIVES ON

Eva finished her term at Chilocco and returned to Fort Sill to live with the Daklugies. She married, and her daughter was born and died in 1910. Eva herself succumbed to tuberculosis in 1911. Robert Geronimo transferred to Carlisle after his father's death and returned to live on the Mescalero Apache reservation. He died in 1966, leaving four children descended from Geronimo. Lenna, who died in 1918, also left descendants.[15] Asa Daklugie, long raised by Geronimo to succeed him, was finally elected acting chief in 1905, taking Geronimo's place as the power behind the throne, as Naiche remained the official chief until his death. The Apaches were officially promised the land at Fort Sill as a permanent home, since the military intended to abandon their frontier posts deemed no longer necessary. Knowing that they were to keep the land, the Apaches had built a profitable cattle operation there. The military changed its mind, however, and decided that it would keep Fort Sill as an artillery training site; it became the artillery school of fire in 1910. Since the military wanted the Apaches off the Fort Sill land, Congress finally passed a law on August 24, 1912, releasing the Apache prisoners of war and appropriating money to buy them land of their own. Arizona still refused to have them, so many of the ex-prisoners went to the Mescalero Apache reservation in New Mexico. Some elected to stay in Oklahoma, and farms were purchased for them in the area of Fort Sill from the heirs of the deceased Comanches and Kiowas who were granted the allotments under the Dawes Severalty Act. Each Apache made his own choice, and 183 chose to move to Mescalero, while 78 remained in Oklahoma. Their cattle were sold and the proceeds were split among them. Of the nearly 400 noncombatant Apaches sent to Florida as prisoners of war, these were all that remained. When they were finally released, they were released into poverty; the Fort Sill Apaches lived on separate farms, unable to act as a community. Those who chose to settle at Mescalero were better able to retain their sense of community, but the lands assigned were few and poor, and they suffered a marked decrease in their lifestyle. After Geronimo's death, the Apaches were finally freed.

Geronimo continues to live in American popular culture, even into the 21st century. There are three towns and numerous streets named for him. There is even a Web application server named Geronimo. And there are songs in the popular music of recent decades that mention Geronimo, one of which is sung by Elton John. Songwriter Michael Martin Murphy wrote "Geronimo's Cadillac," which was subsequently recorded by Cher.

A controversy about Geronimo's remains arose as recently as 2006. In a recently found letter, a member of a Yale secret society, the Skull and Bones, claimed to have removed Geronimo's skull and femur from his grave. Rumor has it that these bones are currently located at The Tomb, the society's headquarters, where members kiss the skull in their own ceremony. In 2006, Harlyn Geronimo, a descendent of the old chief, appealed to President Bush (a former Skull and Bones member) to help him recover Geronimo's remains. While society members think that they have Geronimo's bones, only DNA testing could prove such a thing. In the meantime, other Apache descendents still living near Fort Sill claim that this is a hoax, and that Geronimo's remains have not been disturbed, which is a very strong Apache taboo.[16] On February 17, 2009, Harlyn Geronimo (Geronimo's great grandson) and his family filed a federal lawsuit against the Skull and Bones, Yale University, and the federal government on the 100th anniversary of Geronimo's death. He wants any remains to be returned to his family to be reburied near Geronimo's birthplace in the Gila Wilderness.[17]

What manner of man was Geronimo, and what has been his legacy? First and foremost, he was a man who cared deeply for his family, and who worked hard to provide for them. He also accepted a position of leadership within his band, with all the responsibilities that entailed, and he always endeavored to use his best judgment in taking care of the people of his band. He was a good warrior, self-taught, and was adept at strategy and at figuring out the military styles and strategies of two different countries. His courage was legendary, and let us not forget his power, which was verified and respected by many; it marked him as an extraordinary man.

Geronimo was also a man with weaknesses. He was a gambler by nature, and this may have figured into the success of some of his strategies, although it is most likely that his intelligence, hard work, luck, and lack of trust of the white man made him far more successful than his gambling acumen. His arrogance, weakness for the bottle, and paranoid fear of the White Eyes led to some bad choices, and even caused his death.

Geronimo remains an icon, because he was the best and the last. He maintained his traditional Apache lifestyle, living off the land, far longer than other Native Americans were able to once miners and settlers began flooding the west. He emerged victorious and unscathed from many battles with Mexicans, Americans, and other bands. At the end, with his band whittled down to 30 people, he had the entire U.S. Army chasing him with more than 5,000 soldiers; they never captured him, and had no hope of doing so. He chose surrender in the end. For him, there was nowhere to go, nothing else to do. While Geronimo remained free, the lands around him were taken over by outsiders, and both the landscape and the times changed. His skills at raiding and living off the land were no longer the skills necessary for survival, for there was little enough land left to live off, and punishment for raiding was harsh and inevitable.

He lived to see the World's Fair, ride in a president's inaugural parade, have photographs and postcards made of him, and become a seller of souvenirs. All this he did from captivity, and he ended his life in that state, as a prisoner of war. In the end he became a commodity, as did so many of the Native Americans who were struggling to create a new life on the frontier. He learned some new things: he learned that the Americans had a power stronger than his, and it was due primarily to sheer overwhelming numbers. They never stopped coming; they overran the land. He quickly learned the power of the dollar, a power that the Americans seemed to respect. He became a master of money-making schemes, even as a prisoner of war with very few privileges. It was reputed that when Geronimo died, he had more than $10,000 in the bank.[18] Geronimo, renowned for his courage and mastery of guerilla warfare, was a symbol of his people and of his time.

NOTES

1. P. Aleshire, *The Fox and the Whirlwind: General George Crook and Geronimo: A Paired Biography* (New York: Wiley, 2000), pp. 324–325.

2. Eve Ball, *Indeh: An Apache Odyssey*, with Nora Henn and Lynda Sanchez (Norman: University of Oklahoma Press, 1980), p. 174.

3. Geronimo, *Geronimo's Story of His Life*, transcribed and edited by S. M. Barrett (New York: Duffield & Co., 1915), http://books.google.com/books?id=AvYaAAAAYAAJ, pp. 213–216.

4. Elbridge Ayer Burbank, *Burbank Among the Indians* as told to Ernest Royce (Caxton Press, 1972), http://www.harvard-diggins.org/Burbank/Burbank_Among_The_Indians/Burbank_Among_the_Indians.htm, pp. 12–13.

5. Angie Debo, *Geronimo: The Man, His Time, His Place* (Norman: University of Oklahoma Press, 1976), p. 382.

6. David Roberts, *Once They Moved Like the Wind: Cochise, Geronimo, and the Apache Wars* (New York: Simon & Schuster, 1993), p. 310.

7. Debo, *Geronimo*, p. 387.

8. Debo, *Geronimo*, p. 428.

9. Geronimo, *Geronimo's Story of His Life*, transcribed and edited by S. M. Barrett (New York: Duffield & Co., 1915), http://books.google.com/books?id=AvYaAAAAYAAJ, pp. 211–212.

10. Debo, *Geronimo*, p. 437.

11. Ball, *Indeh*, p. 179.

12. Ball, *Indeh*, p. 181.

13. Debo, *Geronimo*, p. 441.

14. "Old Apache Chief Geronimo Is Dead," *New York Times* (February 18, 1909), http://www.nytimes.com/learning/general/onthisday/bday/0616.html.

15. Sharon Magee, "The Many Wives of Geronimo," *Arizona Highways* (March 2000): p. 21.

16. Mary Annette Pember, "Tomb Raiders," *Diverse: Issues in Higher Education* 24, no. 11 (July 12, 2007): pp. 10–11; Andrew Buncombe, "Geronimo's Family Call on Bush to Help Return His Skeleton," *The Independent* (June 1, 2006), http://news.independent.co.uk/world/americas/article622744.ece.

17. "Kin Sue Elite Yale Secret Society, Claim Geronimo's Remains Stolen," *Arizona Daily Star* (February 19, 2009), p. A3.

18. Burbank, *Burbank Among the Indians*, p. 12.

GLOSSARY

Acculturate—To cause someone to adapt to or adopt the dominant culture

Apacheria—The area traditionally inhabited by the Apaches; roughly, southeastern Arizona, southwestern New Mexico, and northern Mexico

Bedonkohes—The band of Chiricahua Apaches to which Geronimo belonged

Bullroarer—A piece of wood attached to a string that is whirled around to produce a roaring noise

Chihuahua, Mexico—The state in northeastern Mexico that shares a border with the United States

Depredations—Attacking, plundering, looting, and destroying

Encroaching—Intruding on another's territory or rights

Garbed—Wore clothing of a particular kind

Goyahkla—Geronimo's given boyhood name, meaning "He Who Yawns"

Nomadic—Moving seasonally for hunting and gathering

Philanthropic—An organization that promotes the welfare of others; humanitarian or charitable

Rancheria—A semi-permanent group of dwellings for an Apache band

Renegade—A person who abandons their group or who behaves rebelliously

Reparation—Making amends for a wrong by providing payment

Reservation—An area of land set aside for occupation by Native Americans

Shaman—A priest who has access to the spirit world; a person with healing power

Sonora, Mexico—The state in northwestern Mexico that shares a border with the United States

Tizwin—A mild alcoholic beverage or beer traditionally made from fermented corn

Transcontinental—Crossing the entire continent, such as a railway

Tsosch—An Apache cradleboard for holding and carrying babies

Usen—The most powerful Apache diety, known as "Life Giver"

Wikiup—A dome-shaped Native American hut made with a frame covered by brush or grass

SELECTED BIBLIOGRAPHY

BOOKS

Aleshire, P. *The Fox and the Whirlwind: General George Crook and Geronimo: A Paired Biography.* New York: Wiley, 2000.

Ball, E. *Indeh: An Apache Odyssey.* With Nora Henn and Lynda A. Sanchez. Norman: University of Oklahoma Press, 1980.

Ball, E. *In the Days of Victorio: Recollections of a Warm Springs Apache.* Narrated by James Kaywaykla. Tucson: University of Arizona Press, 1970.

Betzinez, J. *I Fought with Geronimo.* With W. S. Nye. Lincoln: University of Nebraska Press, 1959.

Bourke, J. G. *On the Border with Crook.* Lincoln: University of Nebraska Press, 1891.

Davis, B. *The Truth about Geronimo.* Edited by M. M. Quaife. Lincoln: University of Nebraska Press, 1929.

Debo, A. *Geronimo: The Man, His Time, His Place.* Norman: University of Oklahoma Press, 1976.

Gardner, M. L. *Fort Bowie: National Historic Site.* Tucson, AZ: Southwest Parks and Monuments Association, 1994.

Gardner, M. L. *Geronimo: A Biography.* Tucson, AZ: Western National Parks Association, 2006.

Gatewood, C. B. *Lt. Charles Gatewood & His Apache Wars Memoirs.* Edited and with additional text by Louis Kraft. Lincoln: University of Nebraska Press, 2005.

Geronimo. *Geronimo: His Own Story.* As told to S. M. Barrett, newly revised and edited, with an introduction and notes by Frederick Turner. New York: Meridian, 1996.

Goodwin, G. *Western Apache Raiding and Warfare*. From the notes of Grenville Goodwin. Edited by Keith H. Basso. Tucson: University of Arizona Press, 1971.

Haugen, B. *Geronimo: Apache Warrior*. Minneapolis, MN: Compass Point Books, 2006.

Lummis, C. R. *General Crook and the Apache Wars*. Edited by Turbese Lummis Fiske. Flagstaff, AZ: Northland Press, 1966.

Magee, S. S. *Geronimo! Stories of an American Legend*. Phoenix: Arizona Highways Books, 2002.

Mullane, W. H. *Apache Raids: News about Indian Activity in the Southwest as Reported in the Silver City Enterprise, November 1882 through August 1886*. N.p.: William H. Mullane, 1968.

Opler, M. E. *An Apache Life-way: The Economic, Social, and Religious Institutions of the Chiricahua Indians*. Lincoln: University of Nebraska Press, 1941.

Roberts, D. *Once They Moved Like the Wind: Cochise, Geronimo, and the Apache Wars*. New York: Simon & Schuster, 1993.

Robinson, S. *Apache Voices: Their Stories of Survival as Told to Eve Ball*. Albuquerque: University of New Mexico Press, 2000.

Stockel, H. H. *Women of the Apache Nation: Voices of Truth*. Reno: University of Nevada Press, 1991.

Sweeney, E. R. *Cochise: Chiricahua Apache Chief*. Norman: University of Oklahoma Press, 1991.

Sweeney, E. R. *Mangas Coloradas: Chief of the Chiricahua Apaches*. Norman: University of Oklahoma Press, 1998.

Thrapp, D. L. *The Conquest of Apacheria*. Norman: University of Oklahoma Press, 1967.

Turcheneske, J. A. *The Chiricahua Apache Prisoners of War: Fort Sill, 1894–1914*. Niwot: University Press of Colorado, 1977.

Van Orden, J. *Geronimo's Surrender: The 1886 C.S. Fly Photographs*. Tucson: Arizona Historical Society, 1991.

JOURNAL ARTICLES

Clum, J. "Geronimo." *New Mexico Historical Review* 3, no. 1 (January 1928): 1–40.

Clum, J. "Geronimo (Continued)." *New Mexico Historical Review* 3, no. 2 (April 1928): 121–144.

Clum, J. "Geronimo (Continued)." *New Mexico Historical Review* 3, no. 3 (July 1928): 217–264.

Kenoi, S. "A Chiricahua Apache's Account of the Geronimo Campaign of 1886." Recorded by Morris Opler. *The Journal of Arizona History* 27, no. 1 (Spring 1986): 71–90.

"Kin Sue Elite Yale Secret Society, Claim Geronimo's Remains Stolen." *Arizona Daily Star* (February 19, 2009): A3.

Magee, S. S. "The Many Wives of Geronimo." *Arizona Highways* 76, no. 3 (March 2000): 18–21.

Myers, L. "The Enigma of Mangas Coloradas' Death." *New Mexico Historical Review* 41, no. 4 (October 1966): 287–304.

Pearson, J. D., and F. Wesley. "Recalling the Changing Women: Returning Identity to Chiricahua Apache Women and Children." *Journal of the Southwest* 44, no. 3 (Autumn 2002): 259–275.

Pember, M. A. "Tomb Raiders." *Diverse: Issues in Higher Education* 24, no. 11 (July 2007): 10–11.

Sweeney, E. R. "Geronimo & Chatto: Alternative Apache Ways." *Wild West* (August 2007): 30–39.

Sweeney, E. R. "'I Had Lost All': Geronimo and the Carrasco Massacre of 1851." *Journal of Arizona History* 27, no. 1 (Spring 1986): 35–52.

Utley, R. M. "The Bascom Affair: A Reconstruction." *Arizona and the West* 3 (1961): 59–68.

ELECTRONIC SOURCES

Buncombe, A. "Geronimo's Family Call on Bush to Help Return His Skeleton." *The Independent* (June 1, 2006), http://news.independent.co.uk/world/americas/article622744.ece (accessed September 19, 2008).

Burbank, E. A. *Burbank among the Indians.* As told to E. Royce. Caldwell, ID: Caxton Press, 1972. http://www.harvard-diggins.org/Burbank/Burbank_Among_The_Indians/Burbank_Among_the_Indians.htm (accessed September 19, 2008).

Geronimo. *Geronimo: His Own Story.* 1997. http://www.let.rug.nl/usa/B/geronimo/geronixx.htm (accessed September 27, 2008).

Geronimo. *Geronimo's Story of His Life.* Edited by S. M. Barrett. New York: Duffield, 1915. http://books.google.com/books?id=AvYaAAAAYAAJ&dq=geronimo%20story%20life&pg=PR1 (accessed August 26, 2009).

"Old Apache Chief Geronimo Is Dead." *New York Times*, February 18, 1909, http://www.nytimes.com/learning/general/onthisday/bday/0606.html (accessed September 19, 2008).

VIDEOS

Geronimo and the Apache Resistance. A Peace River Films Production for *American Experience*. DVD. Boston: WCBH Educational Foundation, 1988.
We Shall Remain: America through Native Eyes. DVD. Boston: WGBH Educational Foundation, 2009.

HISTORICAL SITES

Fort Bowie National Historical Site (Arizona) http://www.nps.gov/fobo/
Fort Sill, Oklahoma (U.S. Army) http://sill-www.army.mil/
San Carlos Apache Nation http://www.sancarlosapache.com/home.htm

INDEX

About the Author

MARY A. STOUT is a librarian at Pima Community College in Tucson, Arizona, where she has authored a number of books for younger readers about various Native American tribes. Living in Geronimo's backyard has been a bonus, as she and her family have visited many of the places mentioned in the book firsthand.